THE Pocket BOOK OF BOOSH

THE Pocket BOOK OF BOOSH

DESIGNED AND COMPILED BY
Dave Brown

AUTHORS
Noel Fielding
Julian Barratt
Richard Fulcher
Dave Brown
Richard Ayoade
Michael Fielding

With additional contributions from
Oliver Ralfe
Dee Plume

CANON‖GATE

THE POCKET BOOK OF BOOSH

First published in Great Britain as *The Mighty Book of Boosh*
in 2008 by Canongate Books Ltd, 14 High Street,
Edinburgh, EH1 1TE

. This paperback edition first published in 2009 by Canongate Books

British Library Cataloguing-in-Publication Data
A catalogue record for this book is available
on request from the British Library.

ISBN 978 1 84767 414 2

Reproduction by Syntax, Edinburgh

Printed and bound in Great Britain by Butler Tanner & Dennis

www.meetatthegate.com
www.themightyboosh.com
www.imthemoon.tv

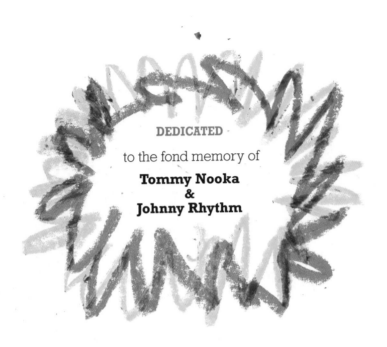

DEDICATED

to the fond memory of

Tommy Nooka
&
Johnny Rhythm

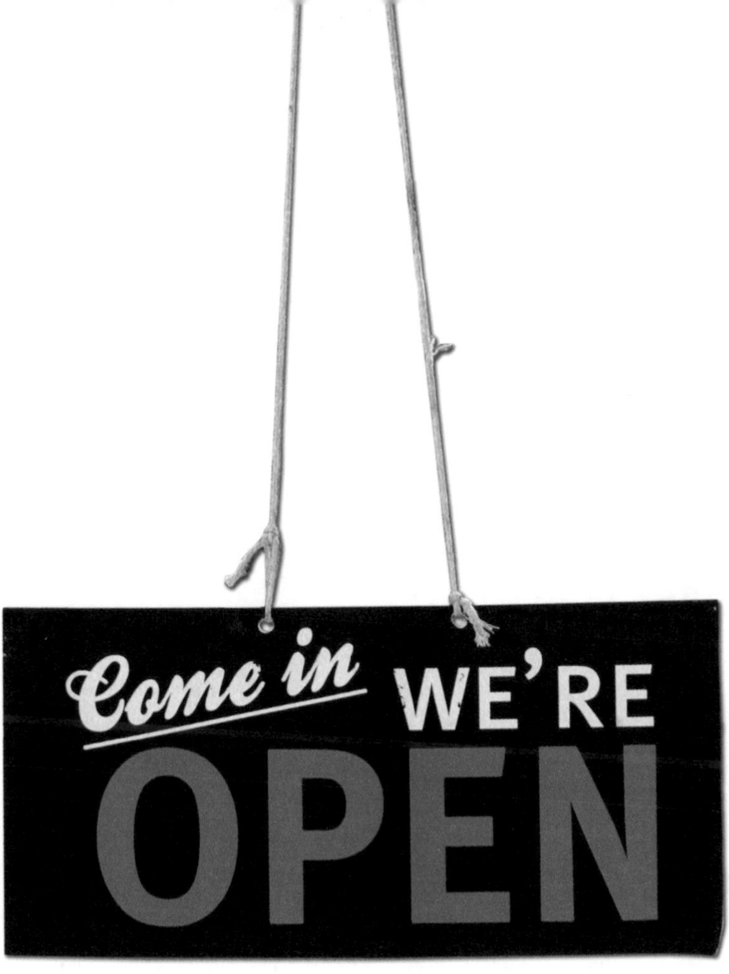
Come in WE'RE
OPEN

This book belongs to

I go by many names....
Some call me
Hannibal Clockparts, others
call me Terry the bat!
Some call me Midge Ure,
others refer to me,
as Mister Master,
Corporal Harry Toenail,
Californian Jimmy Pipe,
some call me Daddy Cuckoo,
whilst others call me
Shiela Tightbone, I have
been known to be called
Roland Purchase or
Tremendous Capricorn
Mathew Nightbus
whilst others sometimes
refer to me as Constant
clench, Susu or Poppy claw
But many do infact know
me as RUDY VAN DISARZIO and
this is MY BOOK! So hands
off or I'll come at you like a
Bag of HAMMERS!

INTRODUCTION
BY HOWARD MOON & VINCE NOIR

H: Just a quick word up front to say hello and welcome to the new, handy, easy-to-wield *Pocket Book of Boosh*.

V: Yeah. Hello.

H: You OK?

V: Yep.

H: Right. So . . . While the larger model got rave reviews all over the world—

V: Except Luxembourg, where it was publicly burnt.

H: Translation problem. Anyhow, generally it was very well received, but one or two people did get back to us saying that its weight was causing upper-arm strain during a long commute.

V: Yes, the problem was it was a bit on the the bulky side, but at the same time it was in danger of getting lost on your larger coffee table. Bit of an annoying 'in-between' size really.

H: Exactly. So here we are with the new, sleek, lightweight, pocket-friendly Boosh book. And we are very excited about it.

V: Well . . . You're more excited than me.

H: What's not to be excited about?

V: I've tried it out and it's rubbish. I put it in my pocket and frankly it ruined the silhouette of my drainpipes.

H: Yeah, but there's no room in your drainpipes for anything. You put them on wet and have them vacuum-sealed at the ankle by a special mechanic.

V: Don't mock my pipes. It's the only future for trousers.

H: That's where you're going wrong, Vince. Now, the readers may have noticed that I cut my own sleek style-corridor through the complex jungle of fashion. And this is where I would like to take the opportunity to offer the readers a chance to invest in the Howard Moon tweed utility pocket suit.

V: What are you doing?

H: Just offering the readers the chance to get involved in my baggy stylings.

V: Don't do that, it's creepy!

H: Look, the deluxe tweed utility suit comes with seventeen handy storage pouches. Perfect for carrying pens, compasses, rare Thelonius Monk albums, First Aid kits, barometers, set squares, you name it. I just want to allow the readers a chance to get involved.

V: The thing is, Howard, that suit makes you look like a fifties wallaby.

H: The pocket is a noble invention. Before pockets, mankind was lost.

V: What, dropping stuff all the time?

H: Exactly. So if we can get back to the introduction—

V: Can I just ask, what's that tie you're wearing in the photo all about?

H: I can't remember, Vince. I probably had an important job interview or something.

V: What, at Rumbelows?

H: No, not at Rumbelows. Anyway, what the hell are you doing buttoning yourself up like a filthy little chimney sweep?

V: I can't remember, it was such a long time ago. I was only eleven.

H: It was a long time ago. They were simpler times back then. There were no tweed utility suits, unfortunately, but there was a primitive charm to life in those days.

V: There were no drainpipes, either. They had been and gone once already. Imagine that.

H: Freaky times, Vince.

V: Well trippy.

H: Cooking apples were illegal.

V: Yep, and giant Alsatians patrolled the streets with crossbows.

H: That's right, and if you were caught drinking alcohol you would be imprisoned inside a Perspex egg and displayed in the town square.

V: Don't remember that.

H: Well, you were young, Vince, so I protected you from the truth of the times.

V: Thanks Howard, I owe you one.

H: I did what anyone would do in my position, Vince. Well, not anyone. People like Spartacus or Mel Gibson. In fact I was quite a hero back then, Vince. Let me tell you about it.

V: Yeah, I've got to go actually.

H: Where?

V: Leroy's making me dinner. We're having pancakes.

H: How come I didn't get an invite?

V: I don't know.

H: Well that's typical Leroy! I invite him round for my bebop chowder evening on Tuesday, then a week later he decides to do pancakes and no invite. Nothing. Not even a text.

V: Well it's nothing to do with me. If you've got a problem with Leroy, speak to him.

H: I will.

V: Good.

H: See you later then.

V: See you later, Mel Gibson.

H: Are you having sweet or savoury?

V: Sweet then savoury.

H: Unbelievable.

You've got a Mighty Boosh

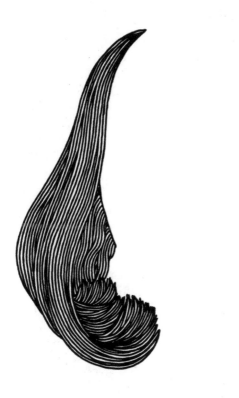

You've got a Mighty Boosh

- Bear eats hitchers thumb.
- Hitcher Vimes scarfe.

HITCHER CHASING VAN.

A WORD FROM HOWARD

Welcome to what will in no doubt be a groundbreaking work of collage/literature. Amidst some of the lesser scribblings of my partner/sidekick Vince Noir will be my ruddy and thrusting poetry and a brief glimpse/teaser at what's been described as my 'shockingly muscular' prose style, think Hemingway meets Coltrane – 'prose so taut you can feel the veins', Tom Paulin. (I like to think of this particular volume as the part of the missile that is jettisoned after launch. My ensuing torrent of novels being the next phase, watch this space.) If this Introduction seems fractured or angular, bear in mind in between sentences I always reach for my trombone (or flugelhorn if it's poetry I am hammering out). Sometimes I compose music and poetry at the same time, a cacophony of creation, munching here on a sausage, smashing out a chord on the piano, ink-stained hands from poetry and criticism. My life is a cacophony of creation, a huge and pullulating comet of art . . . such is the life of Howard Moon, novelist, poet, jazz musician, painter, cycle courier, and after dinner speaker and marsupugilist.

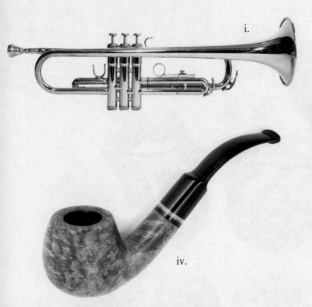

i.

ii.

iv.

How do I keep myself so strong and lithe? I may disclose some of my jazzercise techniques, along with the history of the brass trumpet (figure i), the evolution of the table top globe (figure ii), a generous portion of embossed bookmark designs (figure iii) and I will also be sharing with you my encyclopaedic knowledge of the pipe (figure iv). I will be taking you into my inner psyche via some very modern literary devices.

I will be opening up my psyche via the very underemployed device of stream of consciousness or automatic writing. No editing, no censorship, just raw undiminished Moon. Prepare yourself, clear your mind, indulge in a mantra of choice, pray to whatever gods you hold dear and dive into the plasma pool.

With kindest, deepest, throbbing regards,

iii.

Howard T. J. Moon

FROM VINCE

Hey camden children Vince here
the glitter bug ~~MAYOR~~ of kentish town.
Hope you dig the Boosh book and all
the groovy photos bollo took. skip past
Howards bits though. Well dry. Especially
his chapter on "globes through the ages."
In fact I might have to have a word
with the publishers about that section.
That could easily be replaced with
my POP-UP story about Ace Frehley
the space legend from kiss who saves
the world from evil robotic Jackals
with an uzi that fires glitter
and sequins. Well cool.

VINCE X

GLAM

BOB FOSSIL PROMOTIONS PRESENTS THE FIRST

FOR O

THE ZOONIVERSE M

MAIN

THE ANTIPODEAN
KILLING MACHEAN

212 KILLS, 147 DISEMBOWELMENTS, WANTED IN 1

HOWARD

TOMMY JERRY

FORM

— 5 ROUNDS —

MICKEY THE FIST vs JACKIE THE JAB

ADMISSION 33 EUROS - RESER

FOR TICKETS CALL BOB FOSSIL'S BOX OFFICE ON 0600 123 45678 OR VISIT NABOO'

SHADY UNDERGROUND BOXING COMPETITION

LY IN

N ARENA | SAT. AUG. 24
9:30 P.M.

OUNDS

ILLEROO

FOR EATING A MAN'S FACE RIGHT OFF HIS SKULL

OON

STITUTE

— 5 ROUNDS —

MMY THE REACH VS BOBBY UPPERCUTS

ROS – RINGSIDE 55 EUROS

URCHASE ON LINE AT BOBFOSSILSSEEDYUNDERGROUNDBOXINGCOMPETITION.COM

HEY LOSERS!

THIS IS BOBBY BOB BOB. I LIKE TO RUN THE ZOONIVERSE,
   PLAY GOLF AND TOUCH THINGS THAT ARE SMALL. LET ME TELL
YOU SOMETHING, NUMNUT. IF YOU BOUGHT THIS BOOK
AND YOU ARE DOING THIS THING WHICH I'VE READ ABOUT
CALLED 'READING', THEN YOU ARE A BIGTIME LOSER
WITH A HUMPITY HUMP! THAT'S RIGHT, I SAID IT, AND IF YA DON'T
LIKE IT, GO EAT A NUN SANDWICH!

READING IS DUMB AND ONLY LEADS TO EVIL AND COMMUNISM AND CLOWNS.
   I SHOULD KNOW, CUZ I'VE BEEN . . . I MEAN I AM IN VIET NAM.
HAVE YOU EVER BEEN IN NAM? OF COURSE YOU HAVEN'T,
CUZ YOU'RE READIN' THIS FRIGGIN' BOOK AND YOU'RE NOT OUT THERE
   IN THE BUSH WHERE CHARLIE IS CREEPIN' AROUND ON HIS BELLY
WAITING TO SHOOT YOU IN THE RUMP WITH A BAZOOKA UNTIL YOU SCREAM:
'MOOOOOOOOMMMY!' THAT'S WHY I DON'T READ, I'VE GOTTA
SAVE MY ASS. IF I PICK UP A BOOK, I SWEAR I'M GONNA GET IT IN THE BUTT.
SO LET'S RECAP: READING LEADS TO EVIL, COMMUNISM, CLOWNS,
   AND CHARLIE! NOT THE PINK CHARLIE YOU'LL READ ABOUT LATER IN
THE BOOK . . . WAIT, I MEAN, WON'T READ CUZ I DON'T KNOW WHAT'S IN IT.
SO CLOSE THE BOOK NOW AND COVER YOUR ANUS.
   WOW, I YELLED SO MUCH I THINK I JUST POPPED A VEIN IN MY HEAD.

I'M FEELING WOOZY AND I THINK I HAVE TO SIT . . .
YOU DID THIS TO ME, BOOK!

BOBBY BOB BOB (A NON-READER)

'RIGHT THEN, ARE YOU ALL SETTLED IN AND SITTING COMFORTABLY? THEN LET ME TELL YOU THE STORY OF THE ACTOR AND THE SOCK.'

Once upon a time in a library on the outskirts of Croydon there was a budding amateur dramatist called Terry. Terry was in charge of the Film & Movies section of the library and as he worked his corner every day he dreamt of becoming a huge Hollywood star. Terry knew every book inside out, all the best techniques, and all the actors from Robin Askwith all the way through to Pierce Brosnan.

One day a new book arrived in the Film & Movies section. As he unwrapped it and attempted to file it in alphabetical order in the library's system, Terry noticed that the book had no author. The cover simply read: *The Greatest Actor that Ever Lived*. Curious, Terry opened the book to try to find the author's name, and to his amazement he found no pages inside. *The Greatest Actor that Ever Lived* was just a shell of a book.

Terry looked more closely. Lying inside, where the pages should've been, was a single white sock with a note pinned to it. It read: '*He who wears this sock will become the greatest actor that ever lived.*' Terry couldn't believe what he'd found. All his dreams had come true! He slipped the sock on and as if by magic he started acting like a lunatic. It was incredible. And when he took it off again, he became all hammy like Yul Brynner. The note was right – Terry was going to become the greatest actor that ever lived!

One crisp morning Terry decided to put his skills to the test at an audition for the new *Harold and Kumar* film. As he got dressed that morning, Terry hunted frantically for his magic sock. Where had he put it? He looked high and low, under the stairs, in the garden, at one point he even thought he may have accidentally put it in the DVD case of *Top Gun* and returned it to Blockbusters, but he phoned them and they couldn't find it. Finally, Terry remembered the washing he'd left in the machine. It must be there. Terry started to unload the machine and carefully hang up his freshly washed clothes, one item at a time, until at last, at the bottom of the drum, he found his magic sock. But there was a problem: the sock was no longer white. A pair of red pants had got caught up in the wash and stained it up like a pink wafer.

Terry told himself not to worry. Who cared if the sock was pink? He was just relieved to have found it in time. And so Terry got dressed and rushed off to his audition where he acted the faces off the casting panel. Once Terry had finished, the panel thanked him for his time but explained they wouldn't be giving him the part. Terry was confused and depressed. He'd been brilliant, hadn't he? As he walked slowly home, Terry thought about where it had all gone wrong. The magic sock was supposed to make him the greatest actor that ever lived. The sock, it seemed, had failed him.

As he walked, Terry's depression turned to anger and in a fit of rage he ripped off the pink sock and threw it in the canal. He regretted it instantly though and peered down at the water to see if he could salvage it, only to find his pink-tinted magic sock entangled in the beak of a duck who was swimming quickly away downstream. There was no rescuing it.

A month later, after another tiring day at the library, Terry was watching telly at home when a trailer for the new *Harold and Kumar* film came on the box. Terry sat up straight in his chair. He was desperate to know who had beaten him to the part. The trailer started with a couple walking along a beach arm in arm. As the camera panned out Terry scanned the leading man, until his eye came to rest on two webbed feet and a single sock.

The sock had made the duck a huge star, he'd simply soaked it in some bleach to turn it crispy white again. In the last year alone the duck has appeared in *The Bill*, *Casualty* and is currently playing the new love interest in *Hollyoaks*.

THE END

There are two morals to this story:

Always double-check your white wash to make sure it hasn't been infiltrated by a colourful bitch.

Always try to control your temper, especially when there are ducks around.

Lots of love,

Naboolio
x x x

'BOLLO'S GOTTA BAD FEELIN ABOUT PORN!'

Bollo is big fan of books, books is how Bollo learn to speak in the English man talk. Bollo is gonna get lots of copy of *The Mighty Book of Boosh* and take them into woodland areas and leave them scattered about for animals to read. You may fink this is weird and that Bollo has lost his hairy mind, but let Bollo explain.

The other day, Bollo was taking dog for walk in park, Bollo have a Spaniel, his name is Roger, Roger like to run into woods at back of park. When Bollo let him off lead, he chase about pissin on tree and eating mushroom. All of sudden Roger stop at old magazine buried in leaf. It was old sexy mag all decay and cover in mud. This happen three times now to Roger and this is why Bollo has gotta bad feelin.

Now don't get Bollo wrong, on the whole, Bollo have many a good feelin bout porno, Bollo subscribe to *Monkey Pumper*, *Cheeky Chimps* and Mandrilwives.com. What worry Bollo is that porno is only book you ever see in the woods, it only literature available to woodland animals! This is not good huh? This is why squirrel and fox come into the city.

So, if like Bollo, you fink woodland animal should have wider range of literature available then do as Bollo do and spread some good books about the forest.

Enjoy the book, love and hairy hugs,

Bollo

X

BOB FOSSIL'S A TO Z OF ANIMALS

ANTEATER – Mr Nose Licker

BEAR – The Russian Hairy Carpet Man

CHEETAH – The Zoom Zoom Guy

DINGO – Baby Eater

ELEPHANT – The Grey Leg Face Man

FROG – Mr Green Hoppy Pants

GORILLA – Can't Remember.
Must Consult Talk Box

HOG – Big Bacon Belly Boy

IGUANA – Lime-tailed Slime Time

JACKAL – Yappy Party People

KANGAROO – Little Hairy Pocket Man

LLAMA – Mr Spitmouth

MANATEE – My Wife

NEWT – Get Away From Me, Newt!

OCTOPUS – You Cup-sucking Bastard

PANDAS – The Black & White
Chinese People That
Eat Sticks

QUEEN BEE – Ooh, I'm a Stuck-up
Buzz Baby

RHINOCEROS – Horny Grey
Mud Man

SNAKE – Long Windy Mover

TURTLE – Slow Movey Old Green Fart

UUURANGUTAN – Hairy Orange Men
From Tree Town

VAMPIRE BAT – The Mouth Suck Flyers

WALRUS – Goofy-toothed Slob

X-RAY FISH – Where the Crap Are They?
They Made Me Sterile!

YAK – Hard To Milk Hairy Chinese Guy

ZEBRAS – Stripey Clippity Clop Man

CHILDHOOD TALES FROM THE JUNGLE

BY VINCE NOIR

When I first met Bumbaklaat the Crocodile he was over two hundred years old and was having a documentary made about his long life in the jungle. Bumba was a good storyteller and a wild character, perfect as the subject of a short film. I myself decided to get a job as a runner on the film to earn some pocket money (I was eight years old at the time). I made tea, collected the rushes, and sponged down Bumba in between long takes.

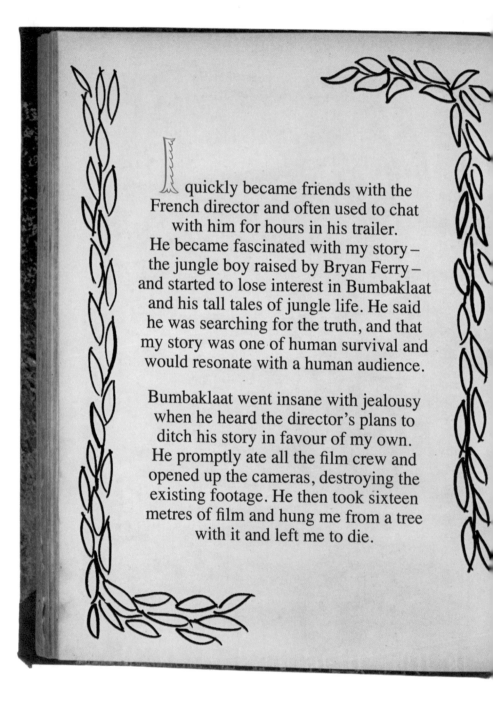

I quickly became friends with the
French director and often used to chat
with him for hours in his trailer.
He became fascinated with my story –
the jungle boy raised by Bryan Ferry –
and started to lose interest in Bumbaklaat
and his tall tales of jungle life. He said
he was searching for the truth, and that
my story was one of human survival and
would resonate with a human audience.

Bumbaklaat went insane with jealousy
when he heard the director's plans to
ditch his story in favour of my own.
He promptly ate all the film crew and
opened up the cameras, destroying the
existing footage. He then took sixteen
metres of film and hung me from a tree
with it and left me to die.

Luckily for me the film melted
in the hot sun and I fell into a hollow
log below. I escaped the ordeal with
broken hips and a punctured lung
but I did survive.

Years later I would often see Bumbaklaat
emerging from the murky waters, bitter
and insane from old age. He would growl
at me, opening his mouth to reveal bits
of film crew in between his teeth, always
wearing the director's bright orange hat
and shouting 'Cut!' and 'There's a hair
in the gate!' and 'Action!' to no one
in particular. I would throw stones at him
from the safety of the river bank and tell
him that I was going to Hollywood to star
in the movies. Bumbaklaat would weep
and try to hurt himself repeatedly.

CALM a LLAMA DOWN
CALM a LLAMA !!!

DEEP DOWN
IN THE OCEAN

BLUE like a
barnicle

TIGHT PLACE

SITTING in THE
laughing at THE MONKEY

arm
ARM

PULLING LIKE A CHINA BOY

KADAWAY KADAWAY KADAWAY
NOISE

boing chi kah masala
boing chi kah masala

ohhhhh   tōōth tooth.

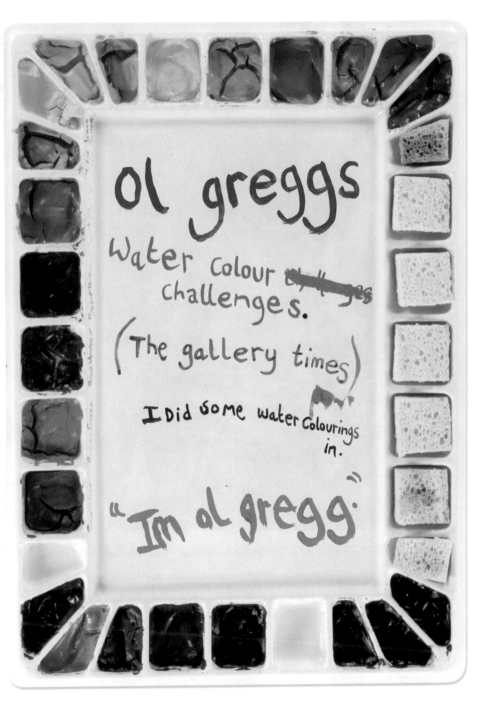

MONGO THE BUTCHERS DOGGY

Thi5 is in fact gauche. I made the upgrade to gauche from watercolours. Watercolours were making me angry.

Thi5 is a drawing of Mongo Mongo, the fisherman's dog. He fell overboard and I saved his life. But his eyes were leaking. He had leaky eye diseases so I paTTEd him with an oAr to make the leaks stop, and it was around this point that he decided to go to sleep for ever, which was bad tIMing.

But he feels nice, when I comes down in the morning for my cereals, as a ruG on the floor.

Ol Gregg likes mini pACks- more Choice that way. I often think of Mongo and think abouT using his skIn on a dog of roughly the same size, aNd how I can bring hiM back to life with gaFFer tape or super glue.

I'm old gregg

Ol' Gregg: Slash

Before I met Howard Moon Slash was my main squeeze.
I was basking on a rock in Los Angeles, next to a used
jonny and some old diet coke cans, and I saw
him jamming on the beach. It was love at first
sight. I used to go to all the Guns 'n' Roses gigs and one
Christmas I baked ten mince pies and hid them
in Slash's tight perm while he was in mid solo for
'Sweet Child O' Mine'. I left and never said goodbye.
I often think about Slash, shaking his black ringlets in
the golden sun, and showering tiny children with my
home baked pastry treats. I got a C in Home Economics,
but I didn't go to catering college, I decided against it for
reasons I don't need to go into right now with you.

I'm Ol' Gregg.

SLASH

Ol' Gregg: Slash-eyes **wide open, eyes** wide shut

The thing about Slash is his hair is always covering his face. Hiding his true beauty. So one night after he nodded out (on opium biscuits), I propped him up and put his hair into a ponytail with **a bungee I f**ound in a deserted Boots. (The Boots only became deserted after I made a call and did a bomb scare. I said there was dynamite **in the Head and** Shoulders.) I'm Ol' Gregg.

Anyway, **Slash** looked like an angel, but there was only one problem for Ol' Gregory. I wanted to paint Slash with his eyes open and his eyes were closed, so I painted some eyes onto two fruit **stickers off** of a pomegranate and I stuck them onto Slash's eyelids. I think it works perfectly well and the false eyes work even better than the originals. So much so I super glued Slash's eyes shut permanently. A gift from Ol' Gregg to Slash my soul mate.

I'm Ol' Gregg.

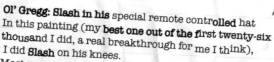

Ol' Gregg: Slash in his special remote contr**olled** hat
In this painting (my **best one out of the** first twenty-six
thousand I did, a real breakthrough for me I think),
I did **Slash** on his knees.

Most people seem to think that Slash is onstage mid-solo,
pulling a rock shape to delight the crowd. But this
isn't the case. He's in the cave weeping.

You see, Slash had be**gun to show** out and act m**ean to**
Ol' Gregory. He started to make things evil. He would
go for a wh**ole minut**e without holding my hand,
and would **try to g**o to places on his own.

(Ice**land and the** library). So I gave Slash a special present
fo**r** his birthday, a new **top hat** that had a remote control
for Gregory to use, and a mechanism inside the brim. That
way, if Slash was trying to be evil to G**regg, I could simp**ly
turn a dial on the remote control and the mechanism would
crush Slash's skull like a watermelon. He soon learnt to
love me again. And in this picture Slash is not lost in music
but having his hat tightene**d to level f**our, which is why he
is on his knees.   A mo**ment lat**er he cried a tear **of blood**
and sc**reamed** out for Axl to help him , so I **had to tak**e him
to level six.

I'm Ol' G**r**egg.

Take ol gregg to paradise City
cos his skin is green
and he sure is pretty.
oh please let me kiss him all over
and hug him
and laug
together and go for walks
I love gregg.

Guns **'n' R**oses **artwork**
This is some artwork that Ol' Gregg did for **Slash's** band.
I told **him th**at I had been doing watercolours
for hobby times and I **was ready to** make the leap
to graphic design times.

Slash seemed a little sceptical so I said that
I would hurt him with fire if he didn't let me have a fair
chance. **(While he was sleeping.) He agreed and I got
down to** work. I did over **396 covers but** they were all
deemed racist by **people so I w**ent back to the drawing
bo**ard and** came up with my masterpiece. Slash seemed
confused and angry and shouted
'What is that? **You kno**w I hate red! Where are the
rest of the band? This is no good, it's embarrassing.'
I think that meant he liked it. I don't **know if they** used
it in the end b**ut it sure was fun to do and made my
tummy fill up with but**terflies as I drew Slash with no
top on for the first time. I'm **Ol' G**regg.

Ol' Gregg: Vinny Toast the talking slice

It ended badly with Slash. Me very upset and him plummeting from a helicopter a 1000ft onto some sharp rocks. I believe he survived and is living inside of a Velvet Revolver now and happy. I always said to Slash, 'You should build a Velvet Revolver and live in it, or a suede Uzi.' But he never listened to Ol' Gregory. Anyway, after he left me I met someone else straight away. (See Slash you thought you could crush Ol' Gregg, but the truth is you meant nothing to me, you were just my sex toy.) I found someone unique and idiosyncratic. Someone who was in fact a piece of toast with mould for eyes and a hole for a mouth called Vinny. Vinny was a caring lover and a sensitive man and Italian. His mother was from the old country, and he would drive me around town on the back of his scooter and buy me cappuccinos and one time Ol' Gregg had a latte with chocolate dust on the foam and the dust went on the end of Ol' Gregg's nose and Vinny gently mopped the dust off of his soft corners and then we kissed and it was so real that everyone outside Bar Italia in Soho clapped and cheered our love and said 'Look, what they've got that's the real deal love. We should reconsider our relationships because they're false and eggy in comparison.' And then we put on our helmets and got on our scooter and then headed off down the road and the bike took off and we flew through pink clouds to a land called 'Paradise City'. Not the cheap place that you talk about Slash, a real place for me and Vinny to go to. And you can never get me back ever, because I'm happy now, more happy than I was with you, so don't even bother calling me on 0208 571 9336 cos I'm not in, I'm at the pink fluffy cloud place with Vinny.

I'm Ol' Gregg. xxxx

A HITCHER'S TALE

WHEN THE HITCHER MET THE RIPPER

It's true I knew The Ripper when he was just
a nipper, but the story don't end there, boy.
Yeah I taught 'im how to stab up and slash out in
a violent frenzy, but in the end the geezer went
wrong so I had to silence 'im. Let me tell you how
it went down as I recall it all those years ago:
It was 1850 (or thereabouts) and there was this
little geezer called Ian. 'Little Ian' we used to
call him. He was a keen lad who used to like
to earn a little bit of extra pocket money
hanging out with me and my green boys,
running errands an' that. We used to send
'im out for Scotch eggs and crab sticks while
we were playing cards or raping.

●

One day we sent 'im out and he never came back. We waited and we waited and finally I went out into the alleyway for a piss. And as I was hosing a dog into a coma, fracturing its skull with my powerful wee-wee jet, I saw Ian – the little git – tryin' ta mug a posh geezer with a knife. The posh bloke weren't 'aving any of it so Ian tried to stab 'im in the belly, but he was feeble and small. All he succeeded in doing really was giving the geezer an extra belt hole. I was totally disgusted with this. If Ian was goin' to roll with me and my crew he was goin' to have to learn the basics. So I put myself away, trundled over and showed 'im how to loosen the man's genitals in one swipe. 'Like this, you rubber johnny,' I said and I gouged out the geezer's eyeball and in one balletic motion tucked it into his watch pocket: 'Now you try.' Ian seemed to pick it up quite naturally and I decided to let 'im live for another hour as a reward.

○

Pretty quickly he became my star student and he was out cutting up everyone in sight: vicars, children, lepers, labradors. Finally it was time for Ian to go his own way so I punched him in the face, threw his shoes in the Thames and told 'im to get away from me or I would widen his head on a rack. He scuttled off into the night like a tiny beetle, but a beetle in a man's outfit. You gotta be cruel to be kind sometimes. Ian had to find his own path. He couldn't spend the rest of his life suckling from my wrinkled green titties.

○

I watched him disappear up the road and finally get knocked down by a horse and cart, and then I went inside and started a fight with a foreign geezer who was – in my opinion – breathing in too much oxygen. 'How dare you?' I said. 'That's London air, you daft frog.' 'I'm not French,' he replied, so I glued his arms to the ceiling. Anyway, this is where the story takes an interesting turn. Twenty-four years later I was coming back to Bethnal Green after selling the Crown Jewels to an Arab gentleman called Cyril when I saw a silhouette lurking in the shadows. What caught my single solo polo peeper was the gentleman seemed to be wearing a top hat just like mine.

○

In fact at first I thought it was my own shadow created from the light of that white gay ball some people refer to as the moon. But the figure started to move around and I was pretty static at the time taking a dump into some bushes. The figure approached another silhouette and took out what appeared to be a dagger, or a screwdriver. Nice, I thought, one of my own boys on the firm. But then the horror struck me. This geezer was pulling a knife out on a lady, either that or a geezer in a dress. I could not believe it. Now I am pure evil but I've got standards. Ladies are out of bounds. You can slap 'em around a bit or shout at 'em, but stabbin 'em? – that is wrong. And this geezer was about to cross the line. I wasted no time at all. I sprinted across the cobbles and blew the character off his feet with a musket I happened to have on my own person.

The lady of the night thanked me in her own individual way (still got the warts to prove it) but here's the shocking part of the tale: after I went through the geezer's pockets for loose change (he weren't quite dead so I took me boot off to finish what I'd started), I raised that red Chelsea boot high above my boatrace and I froze in a state of double decker disgust and confusion.

O

You see, the geezer, on the floor, writhing about in agony, was Ian, the little tit who used to bring me Scotch eggs while I was raping all those years ago. He was The Ripper! Jack they called 'im I think, Jack The Ripper. I said, 'You know you've done wrong in yourself. Now I like to stab up a geezer as much as the next man, but stabbing up a woman? That is not on, son. Anyway, I thought your name was Ian.' He looked up at me with his dying breath and said, 'Well, I thought "Jack The Ripper" had more of a ring to it.' And I agreed, and I finished 'im off with my boot. Took ages in the end because he kept wriggling about on the cobbles like some kind of giant maggot man. Anyway, I cut 'im up into tiny pieces and used 'im as confetti at some kind of posh geezer's wedding. And that's why they never found The Ripper, not because he was clever, or because he out-foxed the police, but because I used 'im as confetti at a wedding.

THE END

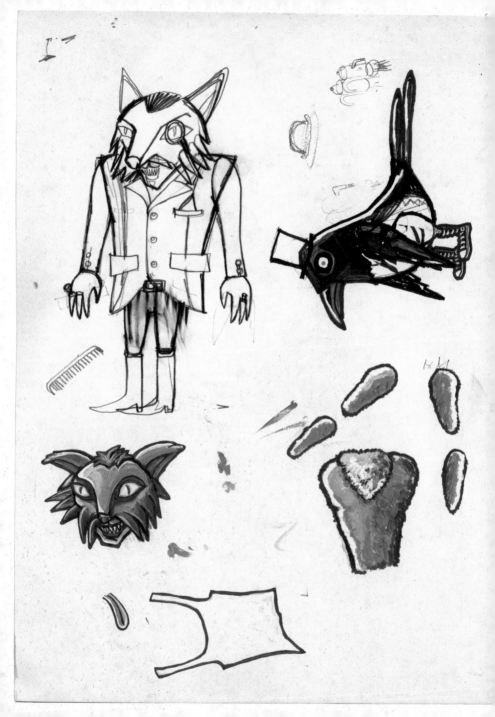

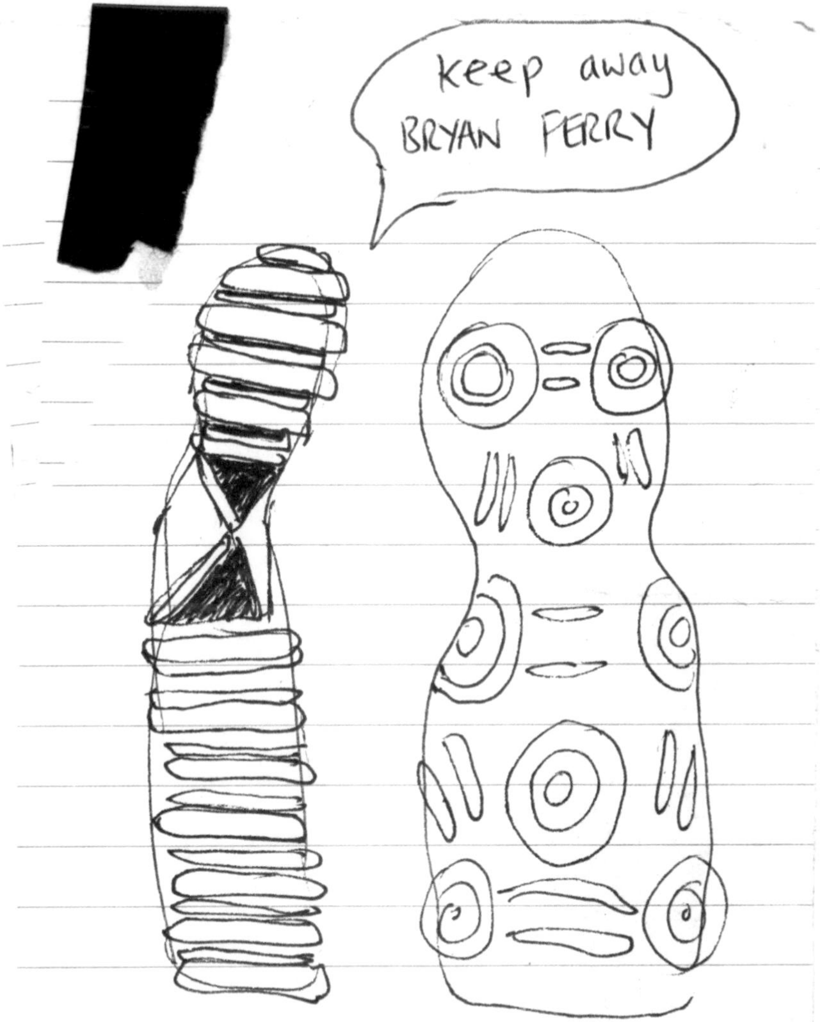

An Outrage at the Shaman Lodge

THE SHAMAN COUNCIL

NAME: TONY HARRISON
TITLE: ENTERTAINMENTS MANAGER
MEMBERSHIP NO: SHC01/2231
EXPIRES BY: 06.09.2056

THE SHAMAN COUNCIL MEMBERSHIP
OFFICIAL MEMBERS CARD

THE SHAMAN COUNCIL

NAME: SABOO
TITLE: CO-UNDER-VICE PRESIDENT
MEMBERSHIP NO: SHC01/2233
EXPIRES BY: 06.09.2057

THE SHAMAN COUNCIL MEMBERSHIP
OFFICIAL MEMBERS CARD

THE SHAMAN COUNCIL

NAME: DENNIS
TITLE: PRESIDENT
MEMBERSHIP NO: SHC01/200
EXPIRES BY: 09.09.2061

THE SHAMAN COUNCIL MEMBERSHIP
OFFICIAL MEMBERS CARD

From: **saboo@sabooworld.com**
Subject: **Shaman club room**
To: **mrandmrstonyharrison@yahoo.com**
Date: **Tue, 17 Jun 23:37**

Dear Tony,
It is with regret that I have to write this e-mail to you. I had hoped
that the recent 'Rodeo' theme night that you 'organised' (I use
quotation marks advisedly) would be a civilised and dignified affair.
Since I doubt that you are able to remember many of the events which
occurred on that sorry eve, allow me to draw your attention to the following:
- The photo of the Shaman Second Eleven Cricket Team was defaced.
- The club room carpet has been heavily soiled. It will have to be replaced.
- You kept lassoing the waitresses.
- The Bucking Bronco has been comprehensively dismantled.
The hire company are demanding a full refund.
- 8,000 euros was 'liberated' from petty cash.
- You and Kirk assaulted the Harry Dean Stanton lookalike.

Needless to say, I cannot let these matters rest. I await your response.

Yours faithfully,
Saboo

From: **mrandmrstonyharrison@yahoo.com**
Subject: **Fwd: Shaman club room**
To: **saboo@sabooworld.com**
Date: **Tue, 17 Jun 23.39**

Dear Saboo
I was personally outraged by the e-mail you sent me. Not only was it one of
the most ill informed pieces of nonsence I have ever had the pleasure to gaze
apon but it was sent to me at 'eleven thirty seven!' You know that my cut off
point for recieving phone calls and e-mails is nine thirty. (I will take a text if my
phone is on silent but only during holidays or floods). I think this is a reasonable rule given that Mrs Harrison has to be up at 'five fifteen' in the morning to do
yoga and open the craft shop. (She does not want to be kept up all night by me
hammering away at the keys to my laptop or vintage typewriter. If I cant sleep
I simply read a magazine or stare at one of my many magic eye posters. The
reason I do this is out of respect for Mrs Harrison (She is after all a former miss
world runner up). Respect my friend,something you seem to know nothing about.

Yes the rodeo night was my idea, an inspired concept that came to me
whilst watching a Lee Van Cleef vehicle. The one with the puma in it that
can fire a gun. (I forget the title). But can I remind you that it is not my
responsability to over see every event once I have set the wagon
wheels in motion. Besides the club room floor was already soiled . (Its so old. I
layed it my self with Dennis back in the eighties). We put that bitch down in one
go, stopping only once for a hula hoop break. As for the second eleven cricket
team why would I deface that ? I was man of the match the day that photo was
taken. Spinning the ball back on its self with my magic pink tubes.

As for dismanteling the bucking Bronco it never bucked all evening,
it just vibrated and slowly moved about the room like a fat mule.(Useless).
And yes Kirk and I did give the Harry Dean Stanton look -alike a
pummeling but only after he became abusive and tried to kiss Dennis.
As Ents manager of the Shaman social club I am deeply offended by
this horrific e-mail and I would like to know two things. Firstly who
the hell do you think you are sunshine? and secondly what is that you even
do in relation to the club. (In which I am one of the founder members).

Yours faithfully, slightly vexed but with some respect.
Tony Harrison. C.B.E

From: **saboo@sabooworld.com**
Subject: **Fwd: Shaman club room**
To: **mrandmrstonyharrison@yahoo.com**
Date: **Wed, 18 Jun 11.03**

Dear Tony,

Thank you for your quick response. I have to say it came as something of a surprise as I assumed you were unable to use a computer keyboard. I shall not embarrass the poor lackey you employed (to type up what I must deduce as being an ill-advised rant into a dictaphone) by pointing out the many typographical and grammatical errors in your recent missive. I will, however, respond to each of your 'points' in turn.

- 11:37 is a perfectly acceptable time to send an e-mail. You were under no obligation to read it straight away. I can't imagine you have anywhere on your person suitable for storing a BlackBerry or an iPhone (I have both) so I assumed you would simply find it in your inbox when you finally shook off the alcohol and woke up.
- While I'll concede that Mrs Harrison is a former Miss World, the 'world' that she comes from is not noted for containing life-forms with very advanced cell structures. I met the Miss World prior to Mrs Harrison: she had no eyes to speak of and breathed through a hole in what I assumed was her back.
- It very much IS your responsibility to oversee the event, especially as YOU 'organised' it. Why don't you stop pointing the finger/tentacle/whatever you call those things coming out of your 'head'?
- How DARE you claim that you put down the club room carpet? As Chief Maintenance Officer, I have laid down every club room carpet over the last three hundred years. And how would you even hold a carpet, you bean bag? Try telling the truth, pal.
- You were not 'man' of the match in that game of cricket: you were the ball.
- I had foreseen that the Bucking Bronco would be a safety hazard. I therefore set it to 'light to moderate buck': the correct speed for risk-free fun.
- Dennis made the first move on Harry Dean Stanton, THEN it turned into a 'Boogie Nights' situation. I saw you goading Kirk on.
- I am Saboo. Who are you?
- I am Chief Maintenance Officer and Co-Under-Vice President to the Committee. A position senior to the Ents Manager. It is unsurprising that you chose not to respond to a number of the points I originally raised in the first e-mail I sent. Perhaps youmight take the time to re-read them? I'm giving you one more chance to explain matters. Do not make me raise further matters that have since come to light. I would much rather that you admitted what you did than for me to have to point out additional indiscretions in writing.

I wish you well, Saboo

From: **mrandmrstonyharrison@yahoo.com**
Subject: **Fwd: Shaman club room**
To: **saboo@sabooworld.com**
Date: **Wed, 18 Jun 13.09**

Have sent you a response to your so-called text! Note the time!
All i will say is that mrs harrison had to skip yoga today and go straight
to the craft centre.

From: **saboo@sabooworld.com**
Subject: **Fwd: Shaman club room**
To: **mrandmrstonyharrison@yahoo.com**
Date: **Wed, 18 Jun 16.05**

We both know that mrs harrison is incapable of 'skipping'. And tell
her that craft shop is low on stock. I have sent you another text.
warm regards, S

From: **mrandmrstonyharrison@yahoo.com**
Subject: **Fwd: Shaman club room**
To: **saboo@sabooworld.com**
Date: **Thur, 19 Jun 10.01**

Ohhhhhhhhhhh here we go. Whats that supposed to mean? 'skipping' !! Is that your attempt at humour? no wonder you put Hale and Pace above Cook and Moore on the comedy wall chart .

Having read your e-mail I can only assume you are on strong medication, cursed or pining for your mummy. Yes I employ someone to type for me but thats because my position as 'ENTS manager' allows me that privilege. I have a small Spanish boy who does all my admin. His English is not amazing but if it's an important e-mail I will run a spell check over it and tease the grammar into shape myself. Likewise if its not important and just a case of knocking out a response to a madman or a junky I leave the document in its raw state, the way Pedro Junior left it.

In response to your absurd allegations: I have plenty of places to store a mobile phone. I sport a european head band. You may have seen the Italian football team doing the same in the championships. A head band that can be stretched out from the temples allowing a blackberry (So 2oo6.) Or an iPhone to be tucked safely in whilst exercising or simply relaxing in town. Secondly you bumbag. Don't hate Mrs Harrison just because she is beautiful.

Thirdly I did indeed lay the carpet in the function room with Dennis. I didn't want to tell you this but the job you did was so shoddy we had to creep back in in the dead of night and start all over again. We didn't tell you because we couldn't bear to see you crying and running around in circles, wetting your knickers.

As for the cricket match, you know I took six for thirty seven that day so let's not pretend otherwise. Also let's not forget you had to make do with preparing the ground and getting the barbeque ready on the sidelines as usual (not even making the first eleven.) Kirk took your place and he was only three hours old. Lastly 'Risk Free Fun' what kind of language is that? The language of a sex case in my opinion. You need to take a look at yourself sunshine.

Yours
Tony Harrison.
p.s. You have clearly lost your way. I've read about this sort of behaviour before in the book 'Helter Skelter'.

From: **saboo@sabooworld.com**
Subject: **Fwd: Shaman club room**
To: **mrandmrstonyharrison@yahoo.com**
Date: **Thur, 19 Jun 19.45**

Tony, Tony, Tony ...
Can I strongly advise that you desist from wearing a headband? Applying any more pressure to your temples may cause your walnut-sized brain more strain than its feeble powers can withstand. My question is: how would you retrieve the phone from the elastic round your clefty bonce? With regards to my text, I was just pointing out an anatomical fact. Neither you nor Mrs Harrison can skip. Perhaps she rolled her way to the craft shop? And, hopefully, via a supply store. Vis-à-vis my comedic tastes, I merely think that SOME of Hale and Pace has been unfairly overlooked (surely you'd agree with that!) and, AS YOU WELL KNOW, I put them JOINT equal third with Cook and Moore, just behind the main guy from The Munsters and Jethro.

With regards your 'arguments', it's as difficult as ever to tell where your arse stops and your head begins. The fact that I organised a barbecue (I received several compliments that day – many thought my home-made burgers were the best they'd ever had) did not stop me from doing some of the best slip fielding of my life. I agreed to go off early while we were fielding to give Kirk some much-needed match time (a courtesy that would never have occurred to you). And, when we went into bat, I ended on an unbeaten 74. You, on the other hand, cannot hold a bat, let alone wield one (whereas my reverse sweep is rightly renowned).

Mrs Harrison is a very attractive example of a certain level of evolution, I'll give you that. Also tell me how, JUST HOW, how IN SODDING HELL DID YOU MANAGE TO LAY A CARPET, YOU PINK SACK OF SHIT? YOU HAVE NO THUMBS!

Please don't force me to cc in Kirk. I'm trying to resolve this in a rational and amicable manner, but trying to talk to you is like watching a demented pig rolling around in ice cream and its own waste.

I await your next ill-governed flail,
Saboo

And by the way – it's not 'junky', it's 'junkie'. I presume you're not William Burroughs (at least he managed to put his whacked-out flights of fancy to some commercial use).

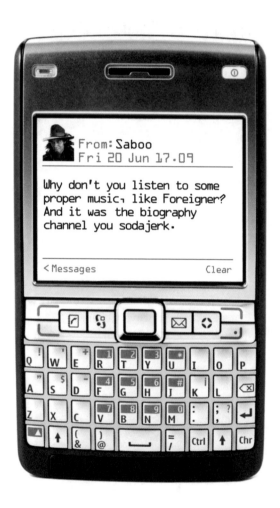

From: **mrandmrstonyharrison@yahoo.com**
Subject: **Fwd: Shaman club room**
To: **saboo@sabooworld.com**
Date: **Sun, 22 Jun 14.39**

Dear Saboo
To be honest the reason I havent sent you a reply to your last e-mail
is because Mrs Harrison and I are having some kitchen work tops fitted
and the place is a mad house. We've got four Polish builders in and
dust everywhere its crazy town. Not just that but the whole weekend
turned into a nightmare. You see we ordered the black granite work
tops with silver marble splashes and these bozos only went and
delivered the silver granite work tops with black marble splashes.
Unbelievable !! This usually would not have been a problem but when
the tops arrived I was next door feeding Mrs Grenolis coy carp. (Just
while she is staying with her daughter in Wimbledon.) So I didn't
actually see them arrive and I had to leave them to it as me and Mrs
Harrison always do a weekly shop on saturday mornings. (Popping into
marks mid week for any extra bits we need.) So we went to Sainsburys
none the wiser only realising the error on our return.) The whole job
had to be re-done. Only the builders started to get stroppy and wave
their arms about. (Dust everywhere.) Now you know as well as I do Mrs
Harrison is allergic to dust and suffers from astma so at this point I
totally lose my rag and you've seen me go. I'm out of control. I said
to the biggest builder 'Listen squire me and my wife are going to
Soho house for dinner, away from this dust factory and if we come back
and the silver granite work tops with the black marble splashes have
not been replaced with the black work tops with silver marbe splashes
I will kick you where the sun dont shine.' Needless to say the whole
situation had been rectified on our return.

Yours Tony Ian Harrison X

From: **saboo@sabooworld.com**

Subject: **Fwd: Shaman club room**

To: **mrandmrstonyharrison@yahoo.com**

Date: **Mon, 23 Jun 10.03**

Dear Tony,

Why didn't you let me know? I would have been happy to pop round and supervise. I've had my ups and downs with builders myself. When I moved into my current abode no work had been done on the interiors since 1973 and I basically had to gut the entire place. But halfway through the contracted work, the builders went on to another job and I was stranded, which meant that I had to stay on the floor of Dennis' study for about four weeks. (I felt so guilty in the end that I bought him a new widescreen HD ready TV.) Plus they'd done the staining of the floor in two sections, so the joins are much darker than I would have ideally liked. Another case in point is that I had a hand-made granite worktop ordered for the bathroom, but when the 'delivery' men finally saw fit to turn up, they couldn't get it up the stairs. So they just sawed it in half! I try to hide the ugly join with my shaving apparatus, but it spoils the sleek effect I was after. And I can't even go into the debacle over the loft conversion. How difficult is it to lay down some chipboard? And I've definitely overspent on the refurbishment. If I sold now, I'd probably make a loss. Which is crazy, because it's a really up-and-coming area (you can be in the centre of town in twenty minutes at a brisk canter and there are some lovely bars springing up just down the road).

Anyway, I'm glad the matter between you and your workforce has been satisfactorily resolved in your favour. You have my sympathies. Hopefully we can reach a similar rapprochement regarding your malfeasances with regards to the club room.

Very best wishes, Saboo

From: **mrandmrstonyharrison@yahoo.com**
Subject: **Fwd: Shaman club room**
To: **saboo@sabooworld.com**
Date: **Mon, 23 Jun 13.07**

Dear Saboo,
For a moment I thought you were going to be man enough to let the whole ugly matter drop but of course you persist in chasing me like an insane dog chases a plate of sausages on wheels. I have explained to you (in sequence) the order of events concerning the 'Rodeo Evening' and yet my explanations appear to mean very little to you. You leave me no choice but to tell you (for the last time) that I am not and never have been responsible for every social event that takes place in the Shaman Club room. The sooner you get that into your thick wide head the better. You are truly captain of all things retarded and the only way you could bring any joy to anyone is if you killed yourself live on YouTube.

Yours, flabbergasted at the levels of your stupidity!
Tony Harrison C.B.E. (Lord of the Dance)
Yes, that's right, I appeared in Riverdance for Flatley when he busted his knee and before you pipe up I received very favourable reviews, so get stuffed!

From: **saboo@sabooworld.com**
Subject: **Fwd: Shaman club room**
To: **mrandmrstonyharrison@yahoo.com**
cc: **dennis@extremesportsmodels.com**
Date: **Mon, 23 Jun 14.02**
> **1 Attachment, 5.2 Kb** (Save)

Right, you anal grape, you leave me no option but to CC Dennis.

Dennis, please find attached all previous e-mails for your attention.

From: **dennis@extremesportsmodels.com**
Subject: **Fwd: Shaman club room**
To: **mrandmrstonyharrison@yahoo.com**
   saboo@sabooworld.com
Date: **Mon, 23 Jun 16.27**

Dearest Tony and Saboo
I have read all previous correspondence. Thank you for making me aware of the situation. I am more than happy to act as a mediator.

Guys, I'm sure we can work this out, there really is no need for all this fighting.
I suggest we meet in the Shaman Social Club over a lager shandy top or two to discuss in more detail. I will get my extreme sports calendar model wife to rustle up a nice potato salad and we will work through these minor issues together without raised voices and any threatening behaviour. I'm sure if we work as a unit we can come to a harmonious understanding. What say you both?

From: **mrandmrstonyharrison@yahoo.com**
Subject: **Fwd: Shaman club room**
To: **dennis@extremesportsmodels.com**
   saboo@sabooworld.com
Date: **Mon, 23 Jun 16.47**

Get lost, Dennis, you ball bag!

P.S. I tried to CC in Kirk in response to you CCing Dennis but he just sent me a link to some farmyard animal porn?

From: **saboo@sabooworld.com**
Subject: **Fwd: Shaman club room**
To: **mrandmrstonyharrison@yahoo.com**
cc: **dennis@extremesportsmodels.com**
Date: **Mon, 23 Jun 16.52**

Yeah, Dennis, you total arse farmer! Mind your own goddamn business!

From: **saboo@sabooworld.com**
Subject: **Fwd: Shaman club room**
To:: **mrandmrstonyharrison@yahoo.com**
Date: **Mon, 23 Jun 16.56**

Can you believe Dennis?! Who the hell does he think he is?

From: **mrandmrstonyharrison@yahoo.com**
Subject: **Fwd: Shaman club room**
To: **saboo@sabooworld.com**
Date: **Mon, 23 Jun 17.02**

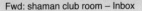

I know, what a complete goon. Fancy meeting up to slag him off and get shitfaced?

From: **saboo@sabooworld.com**
Subject: **Fwd: Shaman club room**
To:: **mrandmrstonyharrison@yahoo.com**
Date: **Mon, 23 Jun 17.16**

Sure thing, H.Man. I will pick you up around 8.

A 20 4 13 19 4 26 21 23
9 NUMBERS TO
4 EXPRESS PAINS
60 PING 5

MY DRIVING INSTRUCTOR

RICH IN
DISGUISE

2 OF THE MOST FUCKED UP PEOPLE
YOU WILL EVER MEET!

BREAD NOSE

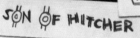

SON OF HITCHER

GIANT JULIAN

CHECK OUT THOSE PINS

NABOO AGED 4

GET IN YOUR SHINEBOX

EDINBURGH BRUTES

EARLY BOOSH

PIPEY.

MIRRORBALLS

PELT THE RABBIT IN HIS BIG WHITE FACE

EDINBURGH 2000

CHICO TIME

LOOK DEEP INTO THE PARKA

DEAR MR PETER JACKSON

Dear **Mr** Peter

Hello, Please allow myself to introduce myself, Myself is Bollo, I am **clever, hard** workin, good **lookin** Gorilla, me very advanced for a primate, I can use over **27** different tools, including black and decker cordless drill.

I love work of Peter Jackson and also love work of your family, I know Michael is **havin a shocker these days but I also know that** he is good man, when Bollo last see my second cousin Bubbles at Auntie Chu**nga funeral he had nofing b**ut good fings to say bout him, although he had drunk 20 Bacardi Breezer and after we speak he did big shit on coffin.

I love lord of flies **film you make,** I specially like beautiful scenery in film, Bollo hope one day to go to Australia to see it for himself.

Enuff of little talk Peter, Bollo cut to chase, the real reason for letter is to tell Peter about Bollo's skills **as actor,** stroke performer, stroke comedian, stroke **dancer, stroke me on my belly coz I like it!!**
(Bollo funny yes? **This is w**hat I do, I try to show Peter more of this stuff in rest of letter).

Bollo have many skill, Bollo can sing, play drum, make tea, I am yellow belt in judo, I **make perfect pot noodle and me can also roll perfect 12 skin** joint blindfolded on magic **carpet in heavy w**inds, I also permed Naboo's hair in the 80's.

cont.

Bollo is 5 feets 9 inch when relax **in hunch** position but 6 foot **5 in heels.** I am 21 stones heavy, but I was wearin big studded belt, leaver jacket and cowboy boots when I weigh myself in Boots. Bollo **have** **Blue eyes, full** head of soft, well groomed Brown **hair, I** also have silver back, it come second in race! It was close r**ace, h**e lost by shoulder blade! (I told you **there was mo**re to come Peter!)

I **fink I end lett**er now Peter, it has been fun imaginin to talk to you in my head and then typin words out on Naboo's typewriter, Bollo's **fingers bit** t**oo** chubby to type, it take me long time **but I like the ding it m**ake at end of each line, it remind me of when I worked on number 38 bus.

Ok Peter, fank you for listenin, I look forward to hearin from you soon, I've got a **good feeling about** this.

Bollo x

p.s The 'x' after my name is a kiss, Bollo would hate Peter to fink I end letters with dirty swear word Bollox.

p.p.s Please find in same envelope as you found letter, some references.

I've got a good feeling about this!

REFERENCE FROM NABOO

All in all I'd say that Bollo is alright, although saying that he did once take the laces out of my trainers to play conkers with Alan next door.

Stick the kettle on Bollo,
Naboo the Enigma.

REFERENCE FROM VINCE NOIR

Bollo is a genius, he straightens my hair like a pro. He knows how to make a proper brew and his cockney mash is second to none. Although he better not be away for too long coz I need him to sew sequins on my new cape and build a rack for my plectrums.

ROCK ON
Vince Noir - Rock and Roll star

REFERENCE FROM BOB FOSSIL

WHO IS THIS BOLLO CHARACTER? IS THIS THE GREY LEG FACE MAN OR THE HAIRY FRENCHMAN? WHAT KIND OF A NAME IS BOLLO ANYWAY? SOUNDS LIKE THE washING POwDER MummY USES TO CLEAN MY PANTIES. LISTEN, IF HE WAS any good I'd definately have made SOME monEY OFF OF HIM BY NOW, SO IF I WERE YOU I'd forget him! oh wAIT A MINUTE, IS THIS THE guy who has the great LUNCH IDEAS?? WHEre ARE MY PANTS MUMMY?

WhatevER
BOBBY BOB BOB BOB KING OF ZOO

REFERENCE FROM HOWARD MOON

To whom it may concern, he may deny it because he's a very modest creature but me and Bollo go way back. I would happily give him a good reference, however, if it's an actor you're looking for then perhaps you need look no further! Are you aware of my work and what I can do? I have taken the liberty of sending you a recent 'piece' of mine directed by the Avante Garde Austrian filmmaker Jurgen Harbourmaster, a one man short film simply called 'Chasing the Sun'. If you don't like this there's always Lucky Break.

Kindest, deepest and thoughtful regards
Howard T. J. Moon

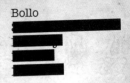

Bollo

Mr Peter Jackson

Dear Peter,

It **been 3 month no**w since I last wrote and Bollo no hear back from Peter. I am finkin that maybe my letter got los**t in post. Nab**oo warned me bout using Royal Mail, he say his ancient mystical method of mind projection **or** carrier eagle is far more be**tter way of delivery let**ter, but, to be honest, I fink that may have freaked Peter out a little bit and so for now I decide to use **paper, envelope and** tiny side of Queen face sticker mefod.

If you no receive Bollo's last letter then you will not know reason I try contact you. I am **Bollo, Britain's leading Gorilla meffod actor, since I type first letter, Bollo** has had lesson on internet and he set up website where Peter can read about him and what he can do, Peter can also download PDF of Bollo CV at W**WW.BOLL**ODENIRO.COM.

Bollo **would lov**e to meet Peter, me no want to seem too pushy and me no mention it in **first letter, Bo**llo have heard through grape line Peter finking of re-making **King Kong, Bollo very exc**ited bout **dis news, me fink** original **film** was total **shit and Bollo know from** Peters work on Die Hard films **that you will** make it full of action and **maybe even Br**uce **Willis** too.

Bollo want Peter to know that he have been to New York before, Bollo also climb Empire State Building, I only went up it on inside though, using normal queue, step **and elevator method rather but I have still been up there so that pretty good for** research huh. I bought an ashtray, keyring and T-shirt for Naboo, he not allowed to come up wiv me coz t**hey think he wa**s terrorist with bomb **in his turban.**

Speak so**on** Peter

Bollo x

(again, **that a kiss not** a bollox)

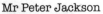

Bollo

Mr Peter Jackson

Dear Jackson

It now been 6 month since Bollo first write letter to Peter bout how good
he is. Me **still hear nuffi**n and Bollo's gettin **many bad feelin** about dis.
Me no wanna sound like that peanut M and M man singin that song wiv
princess Diana boyfriend. **But Bollo getting pretty angry bout Peter bein**
all quiet and no writt**ing and** stuff.

Bo**llo find it h**ard to believe that his **many letter, 2 astral proj**ection,
3 carrier eagle, delivery moth and 1 Addison Lee courier bike all fail
to deliver Bollos letters to Peter.

This is not a threat Mr Jackson but Bo**llo advice Pe**ter to watch National
Geographic channel Wednesday at 9pm. A little documentary called,
'**When Gorilla go** mental and kill human m**an with their massive fist**s'.

Bollo

Bollo

ps Plea**se note th**e lack of kiss

Bollo

Mr Peter Jackson

JACKSON YOU DIRTY LYIN SCRUFFY UGLY DWARF FACED BEARDY
WHALE WATCHIN, BUNGEE JUMPIN, HOBBIT LOVIN LORD OF THE
COCK RING WEARING WANKER!

BOLLO WALK PAST **POSTER ON TUBE TODAY** ADVERTISIN
NEW PETER JACKSON FILM KING FUCKING KONG!!

IM GONNA GET NABOO TO DO SOME VOODOO SHIT ON YOUR
H**AIRY** PUMPKIN ARSE!

BOLLOX

P.S THAT IS A BOLLOX, **A BIG HAIRY O**NE!

Back to back S.K.P

La la la
la la la la

I Am Electro Girl

Jazz bath-tastic!

Howard Moon's
Arctic Journal

Day 1

Seeing as Vince is too busy making snowmen, the task of documenting this journey has fallen to me, Howard Moon. Also, the dictaphone froze. Have packed a sturdy range of tweeds and my favourite trombone. Have a secret supply of sweets sewn into the lining of my jacket. Is this unfair? Surely if it comes to the crunch, the literate one of us should survive. Must sleep now. The devastating cold of the Arctic tundra awaits us . . .

Day 2

Having studied the maps and talked to local Inuits, I believe we are only now four days' travel from the place where the emerald of 'Calahoontoo' was last sighted. The meeting with the Inuits was interesting in many ways. They were very excited to see Vince. There was much singing and dancing and drinking of the local brew. When I arrived the dancing stopped. I obviously inspire fear and awe in the natives, as they retreated into silence and much whispering. When later I played them some bebop on my trombone, they raised their spears at me in a show of respect. Vince offered them his headband and they seemed to cheer up.

The head of the tribe was wearing a strange green amulet that exactly matched Vince's top. They could see he was fascinated by it. Vince said that the head of the tribe shouldn't really be wearing it with furs because of the colour clash, and that he would take it off their hands. Maybe wear it in his next photo shoot. I tried to translate this as best I could, using stick diagrams in the snow until eventually they gave Vince the amulet. After this exchange they all looked at me (for approval I suppose). I nodded and shook their hands and there was much singing and dancing and drinking of the local brew, an interesting beverage made from fermented bear saliva and ground-up owl beaks. Eventually everybody lay in drunken slumber about the camp and we took that as our cue to leave. We thought this better as they had obviously become quite fond of us, especially the head of the tribe who, after having given the amulet to Vince, kept smiling at me and pointing at his groin and doing a strange little dance.

Day 3

We travelled for three days but were forced to camp by the violence of the storms. Vince has built fourteen snowmen outside. He seems determined to build these creatures. Strange; their eerie shapes in the dusk look like sentinels of approaching doom. I wonder why? Supplies low. Must try to sleep and maintain energy for tomorrow. Feel like we're being watched. Maybe it's the snowmen.

Day 4

It's not the snowmen. This morning we awoke to find our provisions eaten. All our sweets and chocolate gone. Stolen in the night by a snowgoose, says Vince. But Vince's spirits are high and his cheeks are rosy. A small toothache is all that ails him. Maintaining his hairdo in sub zero temperatures is apparently quite easy. The ice precludes the use of wax. 'It just stays where it is; genius.' He seems to love it here. I had to get quite brusque and remind him that we are a week from death if this storm does not abate. He agreed but then asked me what abate meant. He seems unable to grasp the consequences or reality of his surroundings. Denial, no doubt. Must keep the truth of our imminent catastrophe from him, his simple mind could not take the shock.

I must weather this cataract in heroic silence.
Such is the burden of greatness and nobility,
I have learnt this from Scott whose diaries
I am presently reading. I tried to talk of Scott
and his many voyages to help pass the time.
But Vince thought I was talking about Terry
Scott the sitcom actor and was amazed that
he'd managed to fit in all these adventures
between filming. I played along out of
kindness. Ignorance is bliss. Never before
have these words rung truer. Onwards,
tomorrow we must cross the Gundaar Pass,
one of the most terrifying ice gorges in the
whole of the Arctic. God be with us.

Day 5
Vince made another snowman, this time
of himself. Where he gets the energy I'll never
know. I asked when he was going
to make a snowman of me and he laughed
for twenty minutes. Ice madness, I think.
I laughed along to make him feel better.

Day 6
Very tired. Can't think straight. Found a pile of empty food supplies in Vince's tent. Though he explained that an enormous kingfisher had brought them into his tent and left them there. I am very tired but I can't be sure he is speaking the truth.

Day 7
Next day. Vince made a double snow sculpture of himself and me standing proud like explorers. I thought he made my eyes a little too small and crooked but other than that it was a fine piece of work. Except for the eyes.

Day 8
Very cold, supplies gone. Only a few essentials left. Sang songs and played trombone to help morale. Vince said he had to leave. I tried to stop him, knowing his exit into this storm would mean his certain death, but he said after my trombone playing death was something he would relish. A joke even as he sacrificed himself for the good of the mission. How noble. He shall be remembered, if not by anyone else at least by me and whomsoever finds these, the last journals of Howard T.J. Moon, Explorer. Poet.

Day 9

I sit in my tent surrounded by snowmen while the storm rages on. Still no sign of Vince. He is gone for good. Dead for sure. Poor little man. I only hope it was quick. My trombone is seizing up in the cold. Have used some of the remaining seal blubber to oil the valves but I can't reach the high C any more. Devastated. All there is now is to wait. Wait and pray that this storm will abate.

Day 10

Storm continues. Supplies gone. Had to eat my tweeds. Must bid farewell to the people in my life. The women who can no longer hope for my return, the people who have trusted in my gifts. My audience, my muses. I must apologise; there will be no more poetry, no more music, but there will be my memory. Trust in that. Howard T.J. Moon. Explorer /poet/ raconteur/ hero/ legend.

Day 11

Wandered blindly through the storm today. Don't know where I am. Pitched my tent for the last time. To think I will never be seen again. I wonder how the world will mourn me? What monuments will they build?

Temples or merely statues? Books and articles obviously, but for how long will I be remembered? Five? Four? Perhaps only three hundred years, perhaps a special day will be set aside. A celebration of art and dance and music that survives long into the future, into a time when man no longer even speaks our language. A time after the great astro-wars of 3012 when perhaps even the origins of the word 'Moon-day' will be lost in the apocalyptic sands of time. Perhaps out of that charred landscape a father and son will appear. 'What is Moon-day, Father?' the young boy will ask in some future tongue. His father will smile:

'It is a day of celebration for a great man. A celebration of his mind and his music.'

'And how might I celebrate this man, Father?'

'Why, by using the sacred pipe!'

At this he will play a jazz solo on a tenor saxophone made from quartz and his son will join in on a perspex clarinet. They will march into the sunset followed by crowds of the bedraggled, playing a futuristic jazz music never heard before ... Had to stop writing this, there is someone outside the tent.

Day 12

I saw a shape coming towards me out of the gloom. As it got closer I realised it was Vince. I opened my arms. 'I thought you were dead!' I said, and he ran past shouting, 'Leg it!' In shock I watched as two dozen angry Inuits came out of the icy gloom holding spears aloft and screaming angrily. I swiftly followed Vince. It turned out he'd misunderstood some cultural signal and found himself in a jacuzzi with all ninety of the elders' wives. A misunderstanding arose that caused him to have to run away at high speed, whence we bumped into each other. We ran and ran but the natives were gaining on us. Eventually we arrived at our base camp. We collapsed at the feet of the snowmen that Vince had built. The natives stopped dead in their tracks when they saw the silhouettes of the forty snowmen standing silently in the gloom. They backed away in fear and disappeared.

'Told you they'd come in handy,' said Vince.

FIRST QUARTER

'When you are in the first quarter of the moon you look like the Phantom of the Opera, you know, the geezer who lives in the theatre and puts Tippex on his face... yeah, he's good, old ying and yang head!'

WAXING GIBBOUS

'I'm not proud of this but you know, it was just a phase I was going through. I got in with the wrong crowd and was drinking heavily. I just felt angry about my situation, what can I say? I've grown since then, spiritually and mentally. I've made progress and I'm very proud of myself!

A phase I was going through! Ha! The moon did a joke!'

THE FULL MOON

'The full moon, the main moon, the chalky white ball bag hanging in the sky like a screwed up letter from a paedophile!'

WANING GIBBOUS

'What does this mean? Waning gibbous? Patrick Moore says it sometimes. I saw him the other day saying it over and over and over, then he dressed up a rabbit like a nurse. He's brilliant!'

THIRD QUARTER

'Did you see Public Enemy at Brixton Academy? They busted that shit out! Raw beats and rhythms, and with Kool Keith supporting, it don't get much better than that. Me and Mars went in a car with blacked-out windows – that is how we roll!'

WAXING CRESCENT

'Jupiter is always waxing lyrical, he loves the sound of his own voice. He told a story the other day about a boy with no face, it went on for ages, it was awful! Saturn was sick on his own rings. Pluto was nonplussed, he told me that when Jupiter starts talking he mentally switches off.'

THE PHASES OF THE MOON

THE NEW MOON

'When you are the moon you can be the new moon or the old moon. I am a really old moon but in comparison to Venus's moon I'm quite new. Venus's moon is really old and can't even rotate properly. He's all jerky and breathes like Darth Vader. People say to me it's not funny to get old but it is quite funny.'

WANING CRESCENT

'Waning crescent moon is the moon that is three quarters light and one quarter in the shadows, but not pitch black. Just a bit dark like when you look at something through a Quality Street wrapper, about that dark.'

郵便はがき

Postcards from Nam

MR BOB FOSSIL

Mommy Fossil,
2 Picket Fence Lane,
Omaha,
Nebraska, UsA

Dear Mommy,
Sorry I haven't **written in 3 years**
but I've been really, really, really
busy. Capt. Vince, made me burn
down a real Vietnamese **village**
and I got captured by the enemy
people. Don't worry, they didn't
torture **me** with sticks or
anything. They did feed me grass
and dry socks and I lost 130
pounds. I can see my spleen now!
How's Dad? Is he still **working on**
the raisin farm?
I kind of gotta go. Sgt. Moon
just blew up my toothbrush.
See you soon, Ma.

Luv, BBB.

Dear Ma Ma,

I just married a really nice girl named 'Long Time'. Sorry I couldn't take her home and show her off but you know, we're in the **middle of a big war.** She really likes me. Most of the time for about 5 minutes, then I don't see her again until the next day when all she does is sleep. Then **we do** the same thing all over again. It's fun, but I get confused a lot. She doesn't like to talk to me and says it tires out her jaw. She said she needed a strong jaw. One day **I fo**llowed her after our 5 minute fun time and she **k**e**pt** visiting friends and stuff. She has a lot of friends. Sometimes she'll yell out

Mummy Fossil,
No. 2 Picket Fence Lane,
Omaha,
Nebraska, UsA

her name on the street and her **friends** will come running up to her. It **must** **be** great to b**e** popular. Oh, I think I hear h**e**r coming.

Love **you,**
BBB x x x

Hi Mom,
It's Bobby **Bob** Bob. I'm writing you from the jungle. **Wait**, I **think** I hear something. Shit. Ahhhh, Boom! Rat-a-**tat**-a-**tat**-a-tat. **Huh?** **Over** here! Hang **on** Ma, just one second. Rat-a-tat-a-a. A**yyy** *!@**&** $%**&** (*Holy Buttcans. I've been hit. Sorry Mommy, that **was** Charlie shelling our position. **Ow!** My guns jam**m**ed--£!&@!% We've got a man down, we've got a man down. Let's **move**, **move** , **move**. So listen, I gotta go Mo**m**my. Wish you we**r**e here.
Kisses,
    Y our B obby. x **X** x

Carte Postale

Mummy Fossil
2 Picket Fence Lane,
Omaha,
Nebraska,
USA

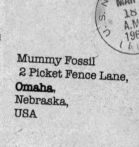

Mom,
What a beautiful day here in Nam. It's really sunny and you can barely smell any dead people. How is Uncle Ja**ck?** Is he still in prison **f**or impersonating a bed? I hope the war ends **soon**.

I can'**t w**ait to come home and touch everybody.

I miss **you mo**re than I miss head lice.

Xxoo**X**xoo
B**o**b

Mummy Fossil
2 Picket Fence Lane,
Omaha,
Nebraska,
USA

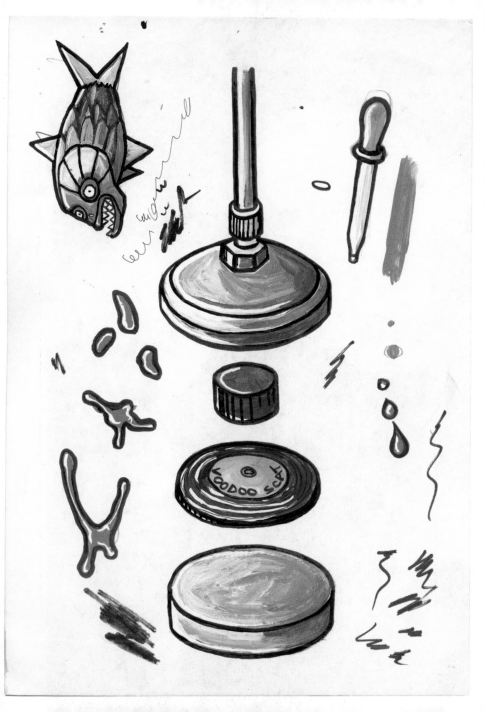

Naboo's Book of Black Magic

La Maison de Dieu

This card looks bad but is actually one of the best in the pack. It basically means you will fall out the window of your flat in the middle of the night screaming. But on the plus side as you hit the pavement face-first you will find that spare key you'd been looking for.

Summary: Good and bad.

Le Diable

This is the one card in the pack you do not want to draw. If you do then you should really hit the Tarot card reader in the eye and make a run for it. This card means the devil will visit you in the night, hairy and fully erect in rape mode. And after the anal pounding, you will be burnt and left in a skip outside your house crying until the milkman finds you at dawn and sexually abuses you a second time.

Summary: You've had a shocker.

Le Pendu

This card is known in the business as the fruitman. If you pull out one of these bitches you will meet the 'lady or man of your dreams' (never really understood that phrase, the 'lady in my dreams' is made from rulers and ice cream). Still, I think it's something to do with love, marriage or pumping.

Summary: Lovefruit.

La Mort

If you get this card you better run for the hills. The skeleton represents toothache or athlete's foot depending on what month it is. The small red house in the background is the skeleton's London flat. He has a nice place in the country but often comes to town for business midweek. Not really, it means Death! Simple as that. You're dead pal – it's over!

Summary: Shinebox. What's done is done. Nothing we could do about it. You picked it. Don't cry, it's embarrassing.

La Roue de Fortune

What the hell's this one? The wheel growing out of the ground on storks' legs. Is this a joke? I've never seen this one before. The blindfolded angel with her tits out. Bollo, have you been on Photoshop again? Maybe it's a new one, they do add new ones sometimes. But it's not a great one, is it? Too much going on really, it's giving me a panic attack.

Summary: Why?

La Force

Oh yes, I like this one, the man giving the lion a Chinese burn. This is a good one. This basically means some kind of change in your life. Not a big change or a sex change. Something small like some new fridge magnets or a different washing powder. The man represents you and the lion represents the washing powder and the red club on the floor represents a cripple.

Summary: Change is good.

XI

LA FORCE

XII

LE CLUB

Le Club

Oh yes, the club with leaves growing out of it. This is the best card in the pack. This means strong erections for life. Only downside being the leaves growing out of your erection can be offputting to some. Although tests show some find it a turn-on, especially the golden leaves. This means a healthy sex life and many children. Ideal for Jaffas or priests.

Summary: Clubcock.

Other Images from the World of Black Magic

This is a page from *The Book of Evil Spirits* by the Great Magus, Lord Crowfoot. In the picture (a famous etching by Aldous Gray) we see the literal visualisation of a magic incantation. The lonely Brave Knight knocks for the Dragon to see if he wants to play out and indulge in a game of Run Outs or Ting Tang Tommy. The Dragon is upset, saying, 'I can't play out. I have chicken pox and my arms have been transformed into branches. Plus my mum is really angry with me cos my BMX got nicked.' The three owls in the background watch the scene unfold and are furious as now the sides will be uneven.

This is Banana Bud Booma Huff Huff
'The Super Magic Man'

It is said that Banana is made from straw and vine leaves and can disappear at will (usually after meals in expensive restaurants). Banana can curse a man on sight simply by ejaculating on a toad and drowning it in a nearby river or lake. Banana is a dark spirit, mischievous and often plays tricks on passers-by, killing their firstborn or blinding them in one eye with a biro, then laughing and running away into the forests. Banana is quite a character. If you happen upon him after midnight the best thing you can do is take him to Megabowl or the ice rink – he thinks these places are sacred realms (the thick nonce).

The Blindfolded Horse

The image of the Blindfolded Horse is a common one in the world of the occult. Another image that you find in books of this nature is the image of the puma in an eyepatch or the eagle in Raybans. All these images are potent symbols of sex magic rituals. 'Sex magic' is the use of sexual interaction to enhance a spell or magic incantation. Orgies can increase the power of the spell by 40 per cent and are often employed by the Magus to make sure the spell works. For example, if the aim is to make someone disappear and only his or her arms have become invisible, a blowey should a least make the torso and head go too.

Monkey Foetus (Good name for a band)

The Monkey Foetus was often grated down by magicians and sprinkled over the heads of the poor in an attempt to bring them some luck financially. Monkey Foetus crumbs in abundance are said to have magical properties and if added to a thick creamy broth and consumed are a powerful aphrodisiac for women and children. Monkey Foetus crumbs can also be added to water stirred into a thick pulp left in the sun to bake and can be used on bricks. It is said that a home made from Monkey Foetus bricks will never fall down or drop in price.

The Evolution
of the Table

Ace Frehley fights the space Jackals.

Our backs were against the wall. We were surrounded by Robotic Jackals as far as the eye could see. "What are we gonna do?" I shouted. "keep cool Vince". Ace replied and pulled out a neon guitar. "Don't worry Vince, check this out." In a flash Ace pointed the fluorescent flying V at the dog faced Bastards and glitter bullets sprayed out into their metallic canine faces. The see-through blood was knee deep but we escaped with our lives. To celebrate I went to the kiss concert that night got myself a lunch box and a small plastic jacket and V.I.P passes back stage to boot. But things got even better. Ace invited me on stage to jam with him and Paul, gene and Peter. We pumped out a throbbing version of "strutter".

And the crowd went mad. I was on
stage with my favourite band and the
crowd were screaming my name. Girls flooded
the stage grabbing at my glitter ball suit
and freshly back combed barnet. I was in
Rock n Roll heaven. That is until one
girl came running at me, side stepped
the security guy and pulled out a laser
gun ready to blast me into kingdom come.
Gene was first to react and wrapped his
unusually long tongue round the girl like
a sea serpent. Paul wasted no time in clubbing
the girl to death with the heel of his silver boot.
As the mad groupie fell to the ground I
couldn't help feeling sorry for her.
That is until she slumped down onto the
stage and pulled off her mask revealing
the face of a shiny jackal. "Must have
been a survivor from earlier." I said.
"That was close." Ace retorted and we
looked at each other, laughed and went
into a sweet version of "Cold Gin."

EWWWHH... GOES LOVELY WITH YER 'AIR, YOUNG LADY.

YESSIR... DIGGIN' IN THE CRATES: HOWARD 'HAWKEYE' MOON.

HEY, HOWARD, THIS CAR BOOT SALE IS GENIUS. CHECK THIS OUT.

A SILVER CAPE...

...AND A PEZ WITH THE FACE OF GARY NUMAN!

MERE TRINKETS, VINCE. THIS, ON THE OTHER HAND, IS A PRETTY RARE FIND. FREDDIE 'DUNEBUG' JEFFERSON.

MASTER OF THE ALTO SAX.

FREDDIE JEFFERSON "blowin' off"

ONLY TWO KNOWN COPIES IN EXISTENCE.

FREDDIE JEFFERSO "blowin 'ff" €1

FREDDIE JEFFERS

FREDDIE

CLEARANCE 1 EURO

CAN YOU TWO STOP MUCKING AROUND? THE LAST THING WE NEED IS SOME CRUSTY OLD RUBBISH BY FREDDIE JAFFACAKES.

WHOA THERE. LOOK AT THIS RUDY AND SPIDER LP!

BET THERE'S SOME TASTY GROOVES ON THIS BABY!

1000 EUROS. CLEARLY OUT OF YOUR BUDGET, MOON.

C'MON, SABOO, I REALLY *NEED* THAT RECORD. HOW ABOUT A *TRADE?*

HOW ABOUT I TRADE YOU A RIDE ON THAT *MOUSTACHE, BIG BOY?*

IGNORE THIS RANDY BALLBAG, THERE'S A FULL *XOOBERON* SOLAR ECLIPSE TONIGHT. HE'S ON HEAT.

SO, A TRADE. WHAT HAVE YOU GOT TO *OFFER,* MOON?

MRS AITCH IS AWAY AND I AM GAGGING...

BONGO NIHONGO RUDY & SPIDER LIVE IN JAPAN. THEIR RAREST ALBUM.

THEY NEARLY DIDN'T MAKE IT...

TO THE LOST TRIBE OF CZUKAY HE IS KNOWN AS THE SHADOWDWELLER.
TO SOME, HIS NAME IS MERELY A WHISPER ON THE LIPS OF THE BELIEVERS AND THE HOLY MEN.
YET, THOSE WHO ARE FLUENT IN THE OLD TONGUE STILL CALL HIM UHULUUHULLURRA.
TO SOME, HE IS KNOWN ONLY AS THE SEEKER.
OTHERS KNOW HIM AS...

MEESTIC BULLSHEET. THAI-STICK MAYBE I COULD USE.

TAI-CHI - TOUCHING THE AIR.

TOUCHING YOURSELF MORE LIKE.

MY **AFRO** IS SPECIALLY SCULPTED TO AMPLIFY SOUND. I CAN **HEAR** A LEAF UNFURL IN THE NEXT VALLEY...

...I CAN CERTAINLY HEAR YOUR IDIOTIC VIBES. I AM **IN TOUCH** WITH THE SPIRITS.

WHY DON'T YOU GET IN TOUCH WITH A **SPANNER** AND HELP ME?

I HAVE **NO UNDERSTANDING** OF THESE VEHICLES AND THEIR WAYS. I WAS BROUGHT UP IN A **MONASTERY**. WE TRAVELLED ONLY **BAREFOOT**.

EVERY TIME WITH THIS... **BULLSHEET**. THE CAR IS A **NERVOUS BREAKDOWN**. WE SUPPOSED TO BE AT THE **AIRPORT!** HOW WE EVER GOING TO GET TO **TOKYO** FOR THE **FESTIVAL ???** **CARLOS SANTANA** WILL ALREADY BE SETTING UP!

PATIENCE, SPIDER. TO THE *PSYCHEDELIC MONKS*, TIME AND SPACE ARE MERELY AN *ILLUSION*. THE BOUNDARIES BETWEEN *CONTINENTS* HAVE NO MEANING TO A MENTAL TRAVELLER SUCH AS I.

THAT'S *NOT* WHAT YOU SAID WHEN YOU GOT *CAUGHT* AT *GATWICK* WITH A GRAM OF CHEEBA UP YOUR *ANUS*, EHHHH? *CRYING* LIKE A *BEEG PURPLE GLOVE PUPPET!*

THAT WAS A *MISUNDERSTANDING* WITH *CUSTOMS AND EXCISE*. I *FORBADE* YOU TO SPEAK OF SUCH MATTERS.

HEH, HEH. *C'MON, RUDY,* LOOSEN UP, EH? DRINK SOME SAKE... A LEETLE BEET OF *GEISHA LOVIN,* Y'KNOW...? WHADDYA SAY, EH?

VERY WELL. PERHAPS THERE IS A WAY.

BUT FIRST, *YOU MUST OPEN YOUR MIND.*

I'M NOT LIKE YOU, RUDY, I AM JUST A *DRUMMER*, YOU CANNOT TURN *COAL* INTO A *DIAMOND*!

THAT IS NOT *STRICTLY TRUE...*

HMMPH... BAD EXAMPLE.

USE THE PRIMAL RHYTHM, SPIDER, *OPEN THE DOOR...*

CUCKUNDOO

WE ARE TRAVELLING IN THE *ASTRAL REALM.* DO NOT FEAR, SPIDER. I SHALL BE YOUR GUIDE.

THIS IS EVEN BETTER THAN *PREMIUM ECONOMY!*

RUDY... WE DID IT! WE'RE HERE! HEY, TOKYO! PREPARE FOR BONGO FURY!!!

hoyrr...

WAIT A MINUTE... WHERE ARE OUR INSTRUMENTS?

←Lost Luggage
Departures

SPIDER DIJON

RUDY VAN DISARZIO

RUDY!! YOU FUCKEENG EEEDIOT!!

IT SEEMS ASTRAL FLIGHT ONLY TRANSPORTS OUR PHYSICAL BODIES, NOT OUR CRUDE TRAPPINGS.

DO NOT WORRY, SPIDER. LUCKILY I ALWAYS CARRY A SET OF PANPIPES IN MY AFRO.

WOW, I BET IT SOUNDS *AMAZING*, THEIR GREATEST ALBUM, EH NABOO? *TURN IT UP!*

IT IS UP. THIS IS IT. TWO HOURS OF SILENCE PUNCTUATED BY RUDY BEING SICK INTO HIS PANPIPES. *IT'S AWFUL.*

YOU GOT IT CHEAP THOUGH, RIGHT, HOWARD?

HOWARD?

EHHWWWW...TAKE IT LIKE A MAN, SELLECK, YOU FILTHY STRUMPET. *THIS*, MY FRIEND...UGH, UGH...

don't say it.

...IS AN *OUTRAAAAGGGE...*

ERM...YEH... PRETTY CHEAP...

Rudy Van DiSarzio's
TALES OF WISDOM

When the eagle speaks it is in the only language he knows, the language of the sky. When I speak it is in the language of music, because it is through music that I fly. Can the eagle play guitar like me? No, he can't, but I can make my guitar sound like the eagle, or a wolf, or a pig!

Inspiration comes when you are least expecting it. You must capture it swiftly or it will drift into ━ oblivion like a moth in the night. ━

One day I sat playing my guitar by a stream looking for inspiration. I looked into the stream and saw a man drowning. He reached out to me and said something but his words were choked with water I reached out to him but he was too far away, so thinking on my feet I unstrapped my guitar and used it to reach him. His fingers grasped at the neck just around the fourth fret and accidentally formed a strange chord

I'd never heard before I immediately snatched my guitar away from him and tried to recreate the chord. After only a few hours I had it, it was a beautiful F sharp minor with a major third. I looked up to thank him but he had gone, so I wrote a song using that very chord in honour of him.

I have played over a billion notes in my life, more notes than there are stars in the heavens, but I have never played anything by Chris De Burgh. — This I will not do. —

I found a young child by the roadside, living on scraps and howling in a subhuman way, and beating on a bloated dead pig with a stick. I watched him for a while and saw he had potential. His sense of rhythm was very advanced for a two-year-old, so I took him under my wing, taught him rhythm and melody. He would eat nothing but mustard, hot French mustard. Then twenty-nine years later, the world met Spider Dijon. Percussionist extraordinaire, but sadly the mustard had caused his brain to degenerate and all he cared about was whisky and women. He became the biggest groupie magnet in all of South America and contracted many diseases which further shrank his brain. Now all he can do is hit things and shout and drink and make the beast with two backs. You can learn how to play the bongos but it is easier to move a mountain three feet to the right than to change the character of a man.

My mother always told me that a woman is like a cactus; succulent and pleasing to the eye but if you touch one, you will suffer a rending of the flesh and subsequent poisoning of the mind, body and nervous system leaving you foaming in the dirt ⚜ like a rabid dog. ⚜

I spent twelve years in the wilderness. I lived off berries and grubs. I needed to get away from the noise of the city and some problems with the law. A wise monk told me that if I wanted to be a true musician I should start by listening to the sounds of nature. So that is what I did, learning to make my guitar sound like an eagle, a mouse, a caterpillar carrying a leaf across gravel, a horse with a cold, a squirrel with hayfever. After I had emulated the calls and grunts of every animal I wondered where I could go next. I looked to the ground at my feet, sand blew amongst my toes. I realised that I needed to move further into the realm of the inanimate, there should be no limit to the sounds I could play. Could I make the sounds of a rock being eroded by a slow-moving stream? It took me three years but I did it. The sound of rain I created too, using only a plectrum, my guitar, my fingers and my nose. One night I was awoken by the sound of a stampede of ten thousand buffalo. It was the loudest sound I had ever heard. I wanted to play that sound but my fingers weren't strong enough, I needed to strengthen them, so every day I would hang from a precipice overhanging a deadly snake-infested ravine. One slip would have meant certain death but I hung off that ledge for seven hours every day.

For four years. My fingers became so strong I could crush quartz in my fist. I could stop dead a charging wildebeest with my forefinger. With my muscular thumb, I could slap a swan's head clean off its neck. I was ready to take on the elements. Could I play the sound of a cloud moving through the heavens? And thunder?

When a man plays the guitar his fingers are entering an infinite musical stream that has run from the beginning of time till now and just as a man can never step into the same river twice, neither can a man play the same notes ⟶ twice. So it is written. ⟶

Even the sound of the wind? It took me another four years but eventually I had all of nature at my fingertips. I could summon any sound, any call of any animal, any sound of nature. I could play the sound of Tuesday evening on Wednesday afternoon. I could simulate the sounds of summer in winter and wake bears from hibernation. But what is music if nobody hears it?

A tree that falls in the forest; though I have heard and can play this sound. (It's actually quite easy.) I realised that all I needed now was an audience. Every night I knew from my observations that the animals of the desert came to the watering hole to bathe and eat, so I waited there and set up my generator to power my amp and just a few lights. I played the music of the desert, so accurate was my portrayal of every nuance of that wilderness that the animals took absolutely no notice of me or my music. I knew at that moment that my work was done. I was ready to return to civilisation and reunite with the world. On my return it was as if I'd never left, people were older and they didn't know who I was. 'I am Rudy van DiSarzio,' I would tell them. 'I play guitar.' They would smile and move away. I had yet to buy clothes and I looked strange, but they knew I spoke the truth for there was fear in their eyes .

Naboo R FRY
the enigma

A Conju...

The puma-faced shaman.

Fossils side kick. A super-
magic man who gets fired
by fossil everyone. But always
saves the day. Soft Voodoo.

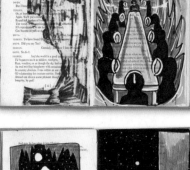

DIXON BAINBRIDGE

A PHOENIX
TOO FREQUENT

A man of action.
A black Roger Moore.

"The wolf attacked me
but fortunately I had a pistol
hidden in my moustache."

Head to foot in tweeds
ginger hair. huge tache.

NEMOID PEACH DADDY MOON

LET ME SHOW YOU HOW I operate!

MUMMA BOOSH

BLUE BERK

RALFE BAND BEARDS

THE K MAN

WINEHOUSE

ON THA BUSES
I HATE YOU BUTLER!!!

EXTREME SPORTS CALENDER MODEL

WHATISBACON?

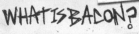
I DID A TUMMY SHAME

MRS RAMSEY

ANTHRAX

MODWOLVES

NANNAGEDDON

NOT IN EXTREME
SPORTS CALENDAR!

THE SAD BROWN SKULL
OF MR FARNABY

SIMON FROM THE
SHOREDITCH SUPERMARKET

ELEANOR'S TOP SEX-PRESSIONS

01 I want to pound you like yesterday's beef.

02 Come dive into Mama's monkeybox.

03 Rrrrrrrrrrrrrrrrrrrrrowwwwwwwwffffff.

04 Take me to a rival planet and turn me into an alien sex slave.

05 Bite me into the next century.

06 Make me a fried egg sandwich, my long order cook.

07 Turn me into a barnacle and let me stick on your love ship.

08 Let me take you to a world where you are 'mouth' and I am 'suck'.

09 Tell me all the things you never told your Uncle Tickly.

10 Tacos, tacos, tacos!

11 Oooh, I'm Scotty... I can't hold it much longer, Captain.

12 Come, my little spaceman, ignite your rocket boosters on my reserve tanks.

13 Tag me with your purple branding iron, you untamed cowboy, you.

14 Let me drop all my loose change in your septic tank and have a giant lookaround.

15 Turn me over and record all over my old DVDs.

16 Pretend I'm Joan of Arc and burn me with your fiery Anglican sceptre.

17 Wash me like I've lived for three years in Rory Bremner's rectum.

18 Ooh, make me learn German and throw me into an endless vat of Black Forest Sauerkraut.

19 Spin me into a wall.

20 Take me into the woods without a compass, stick my face inside an owl and call me your Aunt Sophelia.

SOUP SOUP A TASTY SOUP SOUP A SPICY

CARROT & CORIANDER

CROUTON CROUTON CROUTON

CRUNCHY FRIENDS IN A LIQUID BROTH

CHILLI CHOWDER

I am GAZPACHO Oh

A SUMMER SOUP MMMMM...

I am

FIGHTING MISO MISO

dojo

FIGHTING IN THE

ORIENTAL PRINCE IN THE LAND OF SOUP.

MISO MISO

MISO MISO

The Funk is a ___ creature ___ the
size ___ came ___ the
planet. ___ ___ ___ was
a simple ___ ___ those
mauve titties and ___

___ 1979 the
Day the funk die.
a Cuyen feel. ___ ___
I offered to take him ___ ___
50   I let him live with me here. ___ Daddy.

180 gsm

HOWARD MOON'S JAZZ PORTRAITS

Lightly textured, 25 leaves. Acid free.

"Catching the
Dream."

Howard Moon, 1952

"mmmm That BFlat is salty"

Howard eats JAZZ.
1952.

"I am
Part Trumpet!"
1954.

Nanny Pete

CHRIS DE BATTENBURG
"LADY IN PINK & YELLOW SQUARES!"

RICHY THE BUBBLEGUM BITCH
FEEL MY CHEWY JUSTICE

"ARE THERE CUPS?"
WE ARE HIDEOUS

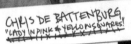

MICKEY THE FIST

NABOOLIO CACTUS

BETAMAX BANDIT

FINISHING GEL, WHAT
IS FINISHING GEL?

GERBACKS
YOUR BUSINESS

CHEESE IS A KIND OF MEAT

ALRIGHT THERE BARRY

PERHAPS THE KING IS CLOSER THAN YOU THINK!

ELECTRO GIRL!

Have you ever seen Brian Ferry

NOT YOU NAAN!

EMMUTANT

DEELEPHANT

60/40 SHED YOUR SKIN!

Tommy Nooka

(Tommy the cheese monk?)

♪♪ Cheese is a form ♪♪
of meat.
A tiny yellow
beef.
♪♪   ♪♪

Tommy Nooka
The cheese priest

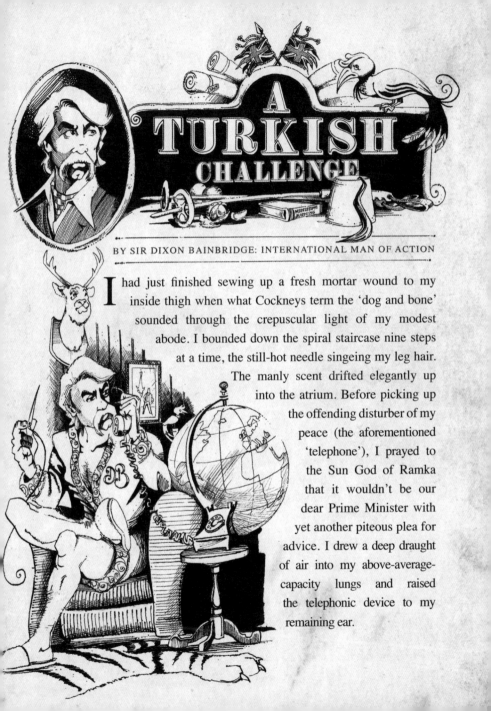

A TURKISH CHALLENGE

BY SIR DIXON BAINBRIDGE: INTERNATIONAL MAN OF ACTION

I had just finished sewing up a fresh mortar wound to my inside thigh when what Cockneys term the 'dog and bone' sounded through the crepuscular light of my modest abode. I bounded down the spiral staircase nine steps at a time, the still-hot needle singeing my leg hair. The manly scent drifted elegantly up into the atrium. Before picking up the offending disturber of my peace (the aforementioned 'telephone'), I prayed to the Sun God of Ramka that it wouldn't be our dear Prime Minister with yet another piteous plea for advice. I drew a deep draught of air into my above-average-capacity lungs and raised the telephonic device to my remaining ear.

'*Mr Bainbridge?*' The voice that addressed me was guttural, ugly and menacing. No doubt a Turk. I could practically smell the paprika, yoghurt and lamb through the receiver.

'*Sir Dixon Bainbridge . . .*' I countered, reminding the cur of my recent inclusion in the New Year's Honours List (the one good piece of advice I gave to that doleful politico). '*State your business, Turk.*'

'*Your wife . . .*'

'*Go on . . .*'

'*I was about to. You interrupted me,*' the strange voice hissed.

'*You're wasting my time . . .*'

'*. . . has been kidnapped!*' He paused. A deadly, viperous pause.

I contemplated pointing out that he had just interrupted me.

The pause lingered, now acrid and black with solemnity.

'*. . . and I'm originally from Staffordshire.*'

I gathered myself.

'*Really?*' I retorted. '*When?*'

'*Well, I was born in 19—*'

'*I didn't mean tell me about Staffordshire, you oaf.*' (Although it does contain Britain's only monkey forest, which, under different circumstances, I would have happily discussed.) '*When do you claim that my wife was kidnapped?*' I boomed.

'*Last night . . .*' the simpleton drizzled. '*I will call with further instructions. Do not try to trace me.*' Click. And with that, the line was dead.

I cannot describe the wave of shock that rushed over me like a pride of geese. To whom, then, had I been making love as the warm morning sun caressed my powerful back? And why had he or she fired a mortar at me? Suddenly, a thought sprung into my mind like a spicy gazelle. Maybe I should try to trace the man who just telephoned. The fool! If he hadn't mentioned it,

I doubt the notion would have ever occurred to me. By lunch I would have forgotten all about my wife, just as I struggle to recall many of the other Mrs Bainbridges or how many florists were felled by my sword last winter. But this was an insult to my character! How dare he forbid me to trace him? He had not the right. This was a challenge!

I went back to my quarters, apologised to the recipient of my amorous employments, obtained an explanation regarding his use of artillery, and packed a few essential items into my knapsack: some sturdy boots; three pairs of brogues; two suits; a dinner jacket (for formal occasions, award ceremonies or should I be hanged); a hunting rifle; some satsumas; a stick (should I need a stick); my lucky skis; the novelisation of *Mississippi Burning* (the original novel left me cold); and a 32-piece set of cutlery.

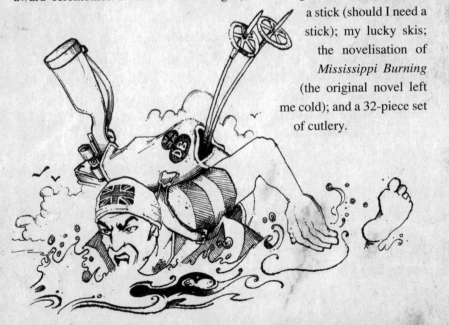

'But how did you know where to go, Bainbridge?' I hear you clamour. Well, dear reader, while on the telephone to this Staffordshire brute, I had heard the unmistakeable sound of the Yellow Keel-Billed Buttonquail or 'Peterson's Bustard' (what natives refer to as 'Ki-Orr-Ahh'). An extremely rare bird, there are only two known to still be in existence. One is in an obscure part of the Brazilian rainforest.The other is stuffed and mounted on the hood of my car. South America it was!

Having been let down by Ryanair more times than I care to mention, I decided it would be best to swim. It was only when I was halfway across the Atlantic that the thought occurred to me: *'Damn it, Bainbridge! You should have used last number redial.'* I consoled myself that I'd just switched over to cable (I had a good all-in-one deal with broadband, telephone and a basic TV package) and I wasn't sure whether my new service provider offered that facility. But I couldn't be sure! And who knows, perhaps the insidious bastard had withheld his number! Could such cunning exist! Why does anyone do that? It makes you so much less likely to pick up the phone. Such are the thoughts that go through one's head when one is delirious with hunger and only one thousand miles into an oceanic adventure to retrieve one's wife!

After what seemed liked months, but might well not have been, but actually was, I neared the shores of Santa Catarina, in the southern sector of Brazil's twenty-six states or *estados* (see Wikipedia for further details). Your hero drifted on to the beach like so much drifting driftwood. I estimated that I had lost three-fifths of my body mass on my aquatic odyssey and decided to allow myself some food. I hungrily devoured one of my satsumas. My strength restored, I set out into the deepest part of the jungle. The path would be perilous. The only other two white men ever to have made this journey were Ant and Dec. And they had had each other. I had only myself! But I was steadfast to find whomever it was I'd set out to look for. I would not be defeated!

Who was I looking for? Did it matter? Perhaps I should enjoy what Brazil had to offer since I was here. How long had it been since I'd killed an ocelot?

Too long! Far too long . . . Ah, Madame Doubt! That many-stockinged, beperfumed mistress and misleader of men! Out, you vile strumpet! I shall not be bent from my course! Like an arrow-shaft, I must be true and on target! My wife! That was it! I had to find my wife! I redoubled my efforts and, after three days' sleep and some hunting (two jaguars and a brace of leopards), I ploughed on.

By now I was deep in the bosom of Brazil. I sharpened my ears, hoping to hear the distinctive 'Hoover'-like sound of Peterson's Bustard. Suddenly, I felt a man's hand on my neck. Was this a flashback to that dread morning of the telephone call? No. It was M'Kambi, my faithful servant from an expedition some years previous when I was involved in my first military coup. The noble savage stood in front of me, his keen eyes widening with delight, his tombstone teeth sparkling with promise. *'Mr Bainbridge, sir,'* he intoned, *'what brings you to this particular branch of Carpet World?'*

'I'm looking for what you natives call Ki-Orr-Ahh but what the White Man calls the Yellow Keel-Billed Buttonquail. But I also saw that you

had some tremendous offers on felt-backed rugs.'

A lively discussion ensued about flat-weaves, underlay, tapestry and stitching techniques. We argued passionately on subjects ranging from the hand-knotted pile carpets that probably originated in southern Central Asia between the third and second millennium BC, via the knotted-pile carpet weaving technology brought to England in the early 16th century by Flemish Calvinists fleeing religious persecution, to the pioneering work of Pierre-Josse Perrot, before ending with a stinging broadside about the short-termism of carpet tiles. We embraced heartily and talked about the old times. Flaying Mexicans, wrestling 'gators in the mud and making boom-boom under the dim beam of the moon. Then he lent me his A–Z and I continued on my quest.

It was two more days before I reached the nesting place of this rare bird. I cursed myself bitterly for weighing myself down with so much carpet. It shouldn't have bought so many. But the deals were so good! My wife, of all people, would surely understand! In view of the sensitive nature of my readership, I will omit my fight to the death with the dreaded Fishmen of the Lower Amazon and the many villages that circumstances forced me to raze to the ground. Suffice to say the call of the bird soon sounded clarion-clear in mine ear and I found myself looking up at a giant bamboo birdcage (suspended from a mighty oak – so incongruous in Brazil!) that held both the Ki-Orr-Ahh and my wife! Which should I save? It would surely be nice to kill and stuff that rare creature and hang it from the rear-view mirror in my Bentley. But pride dictated that I had to at least essay the rescue of my wife. I changed into my dinner jacket and used the stick that I had prudently brought to pole-vault up the some thirty metres to her unjust prison.

Oh, the joy of seeing that handsome woman again! We warmly shook hands as I spent a couple of minutes asking about her general wellbeing. She mentioned that she'd been beaten but, more interestingly, she gave me a notebook filled with marvellous illustrations of the fauna she had noticed during her four-month incarceration (our mutual interest in botany had been one of the reasons I'd freed her from the slave ship where we first met). She apologised for inconveniencing me before gratefully accepting my last satsuma and eating it in one gulp, pip and peel to boot! Then, suddenly, a fearful cry resounded through the very depths of the jungle. I looked up to see an imposing man, dressed in the livery of Staffordshire, swing towards me on a colossal vine. His laugh was like a jackal, his hook-nose (particular to the people of that land-locked county) dripped with ungentlemanly perspiration. Mighty in my anger, I took out my lucky skis, rammed the poles through his heart and watched him tumble to his death.

A single tear of grief fell from my eye. Perhaps, in another age, we might have been friends.

BOB FOSSIL'S GUIDE TO DANCE

PERHAPS THE GREATEST DANCER IN RECENT TIMES SHARES SOME TRADE SECRETS

THE EPILEPTIC CLAM

This is great at parties where you wanna impress your ex-wife (but I never do this!). Rotate your arms left to right in unison in a roundy fashion with your hands pointing up. After a few rotations point down and kick your feet up to the side like they were on a hot fish platter. Rotate to the other side and repeat. If you do it right, you look like you should be hospitalised immediately.

THE DIRECTION HUMPY DANCE

From face forward, turn 90 degrees and point in a direction with a fully extended arm. Join with your other arm. Now this is the tricky part – thrust your hips back and forth towards where you're pointing – it's almost as if you're humping the directions! Now turn 180 degrees in the other direction and repeat.

THE TUMMY RUBBY

Look straight ahead and start rubbin' your tummy while shifting your feet to the beat. Move your hands slow and sexy in a big counterclockwise swirly circle (I don't even know what counterclockwise means). It's almost as if you're rubbing marmite into your belly sack.

THE OSCILL- ATING JERK

One of my favourites! Facing forward, you roll your arms in a tight circle around each other like you're wearing a rotating muff and then flip your arm out to the left, roll some more, then to the right. The beauty is you can be as jerky as you like or just stand still and jerk off . . . Wait, that might have come out wrong.

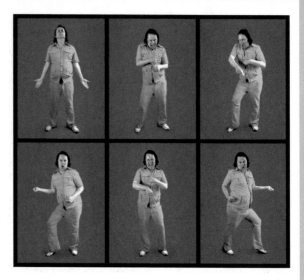

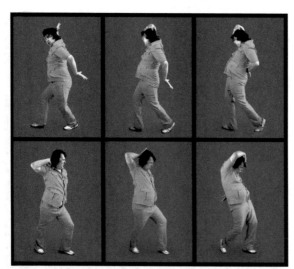

'SHOW ME WHO'S YOUR DADDY'

This is a variation of the Direction Humpy Dance. Same moves, only instead of pointing, you're putting your right hand behind your head and pushing it down to your crotch as if to say, 'Who's your Daddy! . . . I am, you tiger bumming beyatch!'

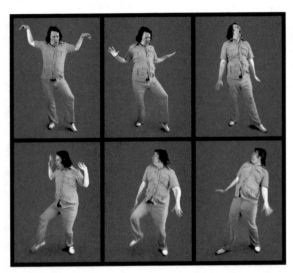

THE KARATE DICK DANCE

Just pretend you're doing that bird move in the Karate Kid movie only instead of kicking, you're flapping and alternating your feet to the beat like some kind of retarded albatross with a skin condition. It's easy, and you'll get attention from police!

THE LACTATING NEPALESE NIPPLE

As you are rocking to the beat, lean back on one foot and lick your fingers at the tips. Rub your nips round and round. Reverse your feet and repeat. The key to this is the staccato-like finger licking – you gotta lick 'em like your fingers are hot pickles!

FEEDING THE CHICKENS

Rocking to the beat from one foot to the other one (one more if you have three feet), punch to the ground but open your hand just as you get to the bottom. This gives the effect that you are angrily feeding chickens. This dance really helps if you don't like poultry.

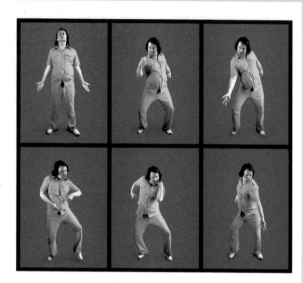

AIR SANDWICH FUN GRAB BOOGIE

While you are gyrating your anus off, grab as many imaginary sandwiches out of the air as you can and stick them into your mouth hole. This dance is great if you're on a diet and think you're actually eating.

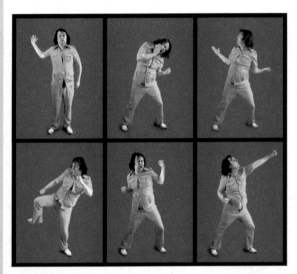

THE CONFUSED SLAPPY DANCE

Slap your face as hard as you can and look confused. Then fight the air as hard as you can with vicious punches and kicks. All of this should be done with the grace of an elk and the violence of an elk.

THE HORNY MILKMAN

Some people say this isn't a dance, it's just humping. It's not. You have to hump to the music. Writhe and grind on top of a special object. Anything you can find around you will do: a file cabinet, desk, ice cream truck, pogo stick or used bag.

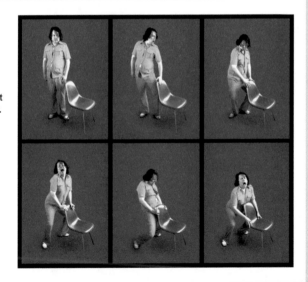

EYE OF THE TIGER GORILLA

BOLLO ♥'s SLY

ROCKY BALBOLLO

RAMBO*LLO*

They sent him on a mission and set him up to fail. But they made one mistake.

They forgot they were dealing with Rambollo

HE'S GOTTA BAD FEELIN ABOUT THIS AND SOON SO WILL THE BADDIES!!!

MARIO KASSAR and ANDREW VAJNA present SYLVESTER STALLONE "RAMBO"

I like shooting things

I ♥ MUM + GUNS

Sly Stallone,
greatest living actor
he should have been man
lead in planet of apes
instead of that gun lovin
monkey kissing wierdo
Bobby Chalton

PLANET OF THE APES
STARRING
SYLVESTER STALLONE
& BOLLO

Imagine a planet
full of apes, that would
be genius! apes in the
bakers, apes in the post
office, apes reading the
news, apes riding bikes
human's in the ZOO!

BOLLO

BOLLO WAZ ERE

Mr Attenborough My hero, 9 months after he visited my mummy I was born, coincidence? hard to say as my mummy was a bit of a tart, but he could be!

my Beautifull Baby, my first love Corretta, Bollo loves redheads, we still friends, no longer lovers we split, Naboo made me chuck her, they didn't get on, I fink he's a bit of a gingist

Bollo loves punk when angry, folk when chilling, and chris de burg when Bollo entertaining lovely lady!

PUNK

NEVER MIND
THE BOLLO
HERE'S THE
Sex Pistols

BOLLO

I get to play Howard's guitar when he goes out, so not that often really.

First Gorilla in space
Bollo would love to
go and see the moon.
could happen Loads of
monkeys have been up
there why not Bollo?

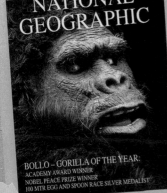

Naballoan
I cant ride a horse.
but I can wear the socks!

Bollo Learned photoshop

Vince's book of EXCUSES FOR BEING LATE VOLUME III

① VINCE'S LIST OF EXCUSES FOR BEING LATE ⚡⚡

HOWARD MOON: WHY ARE YOU LATE?

① I WAS DOING AN ETCHING OF ALAN SUGAR TALKING TO A WHIRL POOL. ✓

② MONTY DON ASKED ME TO GLUE SIM CARDS TO HIS KARATE BELT. ✓

③ ~~I WENT BACK IN TIME TO SAINT TROPEZ AND SHARED OUT SOME MAGIC PEBBLES WITH THE FRENCH LOCALS~~
THIS ONE WONT WORK ↑

④ BRIGITTE BARDOT PUT ME IN A TIME CAPSULE WITH ~~████████~~ A DRAWING OF AN ORANGE CAT HOLDING AN AIR RIFLE. (WHY? I JUST CANT SAY)

⑤ I WAS WITH BRIGITTE BARDOT RE-ENACTING THE NASA MOON LANDING WITH A ~~TALKING~~ SKIPPING ROPE. ↑ TOO MUCH

(ONE OF THESE BARDOT STORYS ONLY.)

⑥ I DRANK OVER A 1000 YAKULTS LAST NIGHT FOR A BET AND WHEN I WOKE UP THIS MORNING I WAS MADE OF SOLID LIGHT.
R (HOWARD WONT GO FOR THIS.)

② **MORE EXCUSES!**

⑦ I WAS HAVING A PENALTY SHOOT-OUT
WITH ~~&~~ THE GHOST OF A FLEA.
↳(THINK THIS IS MY BEST EFFORT ~~YET~~ SO FAR)

⑧ I WAS AUDITIONING FOR THE PART OF
"HAM FACE SILVER LIPS" IN THE MOSQUITO ~~VERS~~
~~&~~ VERSION OF TRON.   (THEY SAID I WAS TOO CAMP.)

⑨ ~~I HAD TOTALLY FORGOTTEN WHAT A TV WAS,
SO SPENT ALL MORNING INVENTING ONE,
FORGETTING THAT IT ALREADY EXISTED, RIGHT
UP UNTIL THE LAST MOMENT WHEN I REMEMBERED
AND FELT FOOLISH.~~

↖ NONSENSE ~~_____~~
COME ON VINCE. THINK.

⑨ I WAS KILLING OWLS WITH DIEGO ~~MARADONNA~~
MARADONNA'S FROZEN SHIN PAD.

⑩ (DOUBLE FIGURES)

I MET A HUMAN ROCKING CHAIR CALLED
CAPTAIN SUCK FORCE.
   ↳MIGHT HAVE TO FOLLOW THIS UP WITH "HE RAPED ME."
      BUT PLAY IT BY EAR.

③
⑨

⟨EXCUSES⟩

⑪ I SPENT ~~THREE~~ HOURS CLIMBING ~~TO THE~~
ON TOP OF THE WORLDS BIGGEST NUROFEN.

⑫ A JAPANESE MAN WITH A FROZEN FACE
BLOCKED ~~MY~~ ^MY^ WIND PIPE WITH TIN FOIL AND
BUCKAROO INSTRUCTIONS.

⑬ (A VISUAL ONE.) COME IN ~~🔲~~ RIDING A GIANT
ON → NOTE PAD ← AND MUMBLE " SPACE SAUCE" OVER
WHEELS AND OVER THEN START A FIGHT WITH AN
INVISIBLE DOCTOR.

⑭ ~~(scribbled out text)~~

A NUMBER SEVEN ~~#~~ THREATENED
ME WITH A ~~CANNON~~. ~~SAUSAGE~~. TENNIS BALL.

⑮ WENT OUT LAST NIGHT WITH MY FRIENDS
MELVIS , LADYBIRD AND WILLY BORREL AND
I HAVEN'T BEEN TO SLEEP YET.

⑯ I WAS WITH NANNY BARCODE → SOUNDS A BIT
CONTRIVED

Mod Wolves in tight Velvet suits.
with Back combed huge hair.

KILLEROO

VINCE

Hi welcome to the show. I write it
and direct it and I shoot it. I work
all the cameras with long poles...

HOWARD WALKS INTO SHOT.

                HOWARD
    What are you doing?

                VINCE
    Just introducing the show.

                HOWARD
    Listen don't start showing out.

                VINCE
    Or what?

                HOWARD
    Or I'll I'll come at you. Like the
    northern bullet. You won't know
    what's happening. I'll Put a move on
    you.

                VINCE
    I'll felt your moves; very flimsey.
    Like being caressed by a natural
    yogurt.

                HOWARD
    They're my old moves. I've got new
    powerful moves now. I'm gonna take
    you to the land of hurt. Take you
    out for a meal with Mr and Mrs pain.

HOWARD STARTS DANCING ABOUT. VINCE STANDS UP BORED.

                VINCE
    Come on then. Bring it on.

HOWARD TOUCHES VINCE ON THE ARM.

                VINCE (CONT'D)
    What was that? Nothing.

                HOWARD
    That move is known as the vibrating
    palm. You feel alright now. But two
    hours from now. You'll go to a shop.
    Buy a hat. It won't suit you ! Oh
    baby. Feel the power of my move.

                VINCE
    Don't be ridiculous . All hats suit
    me. my hair's a hat.

A Trumpet Full of Memories

Howard Moon: Jazz Detective

1

I looked down at the cold body of Miriam 'Toots' Pennybaker. In life she had been hot, but now she was cold. Cold as F minor on a Monday morning. I took out my trumpet and released some sad notes into the room. Miriam stared back, unmoved. I blew a high C. Still nothing. There was a time when she would have joined me. She had a voice that was like burning silk and she was built to last. Unfortunately someone had loosened her neck so there would be no more sweet harmonies from Miriam.

The curtains twitched in the morning air. It could have been the hot blasts from my trumpet, either way I noticed the window was open and there was something on the window ledge, glittering. The mouthpiece of a trumpet. And it wasn't mine. I picked it up. Whoever she had been with the night before was a horn player. A nine by six Boosey mouthpiece, made in Germany, gold plated. There was only one person I knew of in Stoke Newington who blew a Boosey of this particular width. Freddy 'Fire-lips' McGroody, but he was in prison for exposing himself. Looked like I would have to pay a visit to my old friend Lester Corncrake. I pocketed the blow piece, packed away my trumpet and set off. Miriam didn't say goodbye. She'd been strangled to death and wanted to save her voice.

Lester was an old-timer from New Orleans, who repaired musical instruments and drank neat rum. His days of playing jazz were over. He was blind too and said strange things. Some people said he was not all there and should bathe more, but I liked him. It was noon when I arrived at his one-room repair shack. He was sat out front on the porch in a rocking chair, smoking a pipe and repairing the rusty valves of a 1929 C-curve saxophone. I stood and watched him for a moment. I liked to watch him work. His yellow fingers moved slowly but surely over the keys. Behind the ever present sunglasses his sightless eyes were running over an imaginary landscape of notes. Lester had been a jazz musician par excellence before the war but he'd lost his sight in an accident on board a ship in the Gulf of Kiam. Luckily his other senses had increased in sensitivity to compensate. Especially his nose for intrigue.

'Hi there, Lester.'

There was barely a pause.

'Philip Desouza as I live and breathe.'

'It's Howard.'

'Howard?'

'Howard Moon.'

'Oh Howard, of course. How the hell are ya?'

'Pretty good, Lester. Pretty good.'

'What brings you to these parts in the middle of the night?'

I squinted up at the midday sun and chose to ignore the discrepancy. 'Oh, just a question that's been keeping me up, crawling about my skull like a blind scorpion. Can't get to sleep, Lester. Maybe you can help.'

'What's on your mind, Howard?'

'You know what this is?' I held out the mouthpiece. He reached out and grasped it, rotated it deftly in between his long stained fingers, smelt it and listened to it, then rolled it on his thigh.

'A nine by six Boosey trumpet mouthpiece, made in Berlin in 1936, one of only a hundred. Very nice. Yours?'

'Not my style, Lester. I use a Hudson four by one. It's light and lets me hit the high notes at speed. The Boosey is fast but it's unwieldy. Do you know anyone who blows one?'

'Very rare, Howard. A notoriously difficult mouthpiece. Like blowing through solid quartz. Need a pair of lungs on ya like duffel bags to blow this baby, and an embouchure like a hoop of steel.'

'Yeah,' I said, casually.

'Hell of a width, hell of an embouchure. Only three people in this town I know with an embouchure stiff enough to handle a nine by six Boosey.'

'And who might they be?'

'Well now. There's Freddy "Fire-lips" McGroody, Hot "Wee Wee" Jefferson and Herbie Bones. Yep, I reckon they're the only three who could handle this baby.' He handed me back the mouthpiece.

'Thanks a lot, Lester.'

'Pleasure, Howard.'

'By the way, do you remember Miriam Pennybaker?'

He laughed. 'Toots? Hell of a singer . . .' He let out a big sigh full of pipe smoke and regret, 'Hell of a woman.' He looked like he'd been somewhere with Miriam once upon a time. I felt bad. I put my hand on his shoulder.

Lester leapt up and adopted a karate stance. 'Who's that touching me?!' He stood there for a moment. The end of his pipe fell off.

'Easy, Lester, it's still me. Howard.'

'Oh, right.' He sat back down. 'Thought it was a pervert. They come out after dark, Howard. Gotta watch out for them.'

'Yep. I hear you.' The sun beat down upon us for a few moments.

'Jeez, this is one hot night.' He mopped his forehead with an old dishcloth, a stray baked bean now hanging from his eyebrow. 'So, what's Miriam up to these days, anyhow?'

The hope in his voice made him look ten years younger. I swallowed and let him have it. 'Sorry to inform you, but she just played her last set at the Paradise, my friend. Singing for the big man now.'

It was hard to read him. The information took a while to sink in. The baked bean dropped to the floor silently.

'That's a shame, Howard. A real shame. A crying shame.'

'Sure is.'

'Hell of a lady. Had a smell to her, like deep-fried cactus. Like a mangrove swamp filled with candyfloss, you remember?'

'I never got that close to her, Lester.'

'Well, you could smell it from fifteen feet away! Used to drive me insane. Mind you, my senses are unusually sensitive on account of this blindness I is suffering under.'

'I know, Lester.'

'Sometimes I can smell lightning three days away. I can hear a sunset, feel the shadow of a cat on my legs . . . You get me?'

I'd heard all this before. I tipped my hat pointlessly. 'Be seeing you, Lester.'

'Howard?'

I stopped. What now?

'If Miriam's playing anywhere else in the near future, be sure and give me a call. Be great to hear her sing again.'

I wondered what he meant by this. Lester was a difficult goose to cook. Was he really deaf? Was he even blind? One thing for sure: he wasn't stupid. Or was he? Some said he was, many did; in fact I was the only person who held to the contrary. I made a mental note to look into it.

'No, Lester. She's dead!'

I said it slowly, letting the words move into his ear one at a time like tired mice.

'Dead?'

'Yes.'

'Oh, I see. Right.' He frowned.

I left him sucking on his pipe stem and dreaming his dreams. Lester was all set for jazz stardom, way back when, but got involved with a bad woman. That can happen to a man. I knew, I'd been involved with some bad women in my time. And some bad men too, during a short gay phase in Spain, but mainly it was women. Bad and gone. Now all there was, was me. I liked it that way, just me and a trumpet full of memories.

2

As I trudged down Church Street my mind got to thinking. Who could have wanted Miriam dead? I knew Freddy Fire-lips from way back. We used to play together in the Mustard Brothers. He had a mouth on him but no muscle. He wouldn't hurt a fly. And I'm sure Hot Wee-Wee Jefferson was out of town at the GU clinic. But Herbie Bones? I'd heard the name. I made it my business to know the names of every horn player in town. I knew he was supposed to be good, but I'd never heard him play. Perhaps I was getting out of touch. I picked up the listings in a local grocer's and found he was playing at the Blue Aubergine that night. It was 3 o'clock. I decided I was gonna cook, sleep and be ready for what was gonna be a difficult night. I bought some artichokes and Parma ham, cream, chives and mustard, paprika, olive oil and walnuts and a whisk. I liked to eat good; it helped me to think good.

I ate in my apartment with the window open, thinking of Miriam, all the way across town in her apartment with her window open, not thinking of anything. I took out my trumpet and sailed some tall notes across the rooftops. It was hard. I'd spilled some cream on my trumpet and it was making the E's gurgle. I felt suddenly tired, so I ironed my corduroy suit, set my alarm and fell asleep to *Countdown*.

3

The Blue Aubergine was just opening when I arrived about 18:30. I found a quiet corner and settled in, ordered a rum and Coke, donned my shades and watched the band.

The first set started out OK. The bass player and drummer struck up a reasonable conversation in three-four time, nothing fancy. The keyboard player hung a few chords up to dry and it was fine, passed the time, but then some kid got up on flugelhorn and ruined it with a C sharp minor scale. The band were in B major. He tried to escape the embarrassment via an F diminished, but slipped and fell out the window on to an A flat. The band stopped playing. I threw my hat at him. I stepped up.

'Move aside, kid. Let me show you a few moves.'

I stepped up to the mic, screwed in my Hudson mouthpiece, counted in the band and blew. The place began to jump. People called out, 'Stop', 'Yeah', 'No', 'Shit', everyone was feeling it. The kid slunk off like a bad smell. I picked up that room like a cheap hanky and mopped my brow with it, squeezed it out into a glass and made the kid drink the salty leftovers. I was on a roll. The band were burning something hot underneath my horn and I was sizzling on top of it like a sausage, a sausage made from jazz meat.

I played every note there was and even some that weren't. Time passed but I was inside the cauldron, I was a burning bebop beast. Sweat was pouring off me, long strings of saliva were hanging out of the end of my trumpet and forming a pool at my feet. But I didn't care. When it took me I gave in. No point fighting, the juju was up inside my horn. My fingers were just doin' what it told them to do, and fast. My body was twisting like a spring stag, my legs were buckling and twirling, my elbows a hummingbird blur. The duende had got me. Was commanding me. I was vaguely aware of sounds coming from the audience. Dim screams and howls. A woman being sick. A man fell over and yelled for it to stop, but these noises were coming from far away, a million miles away, in another world. I was floating though the galaxy of notes on a giant trumpet made of gold! Blowing, blowing, blowing. Blowing the eyebrows off the face of God!

Lots of people said I could stop time with my horn. They said it made time go slower than molasses in Moscow. They were just being kind because when I looked up, it was 8:37 pm. I'd been soloing for two hours solid. The drummer was exhausted and was sitting on the edge of the stage smoking, the bass player had lost control of his legs and was lying face down under the piano. Maybe he'd slipped on the spit.

The pianist was nowhere to be seen. Through the blur of the sweat and the lights I noticed a heavyset man in a bottle green suit standing by the bar, watching. He had on a pork pie hat and was sporting a goatee. I blew a high C and stepped down off the stage. I was dripping with sweat, steam was coming off me like a racehorse. One man applauded slowly. It was Herbie Bones.

As I got out from under the light and into the crowd I saw that he was the crowd.

'Looks like you've cleared the room again, Moon.'

'Too much for some people. See you stayed though. See something you like? Come to steal my new chops?'

'No chops I saw worth stealin'. They were thin chops, Moon. Thin, like veal. And old.'

'Where's your chops then?'

He pointed to his head. 'Here.' Then his hands. 'And here. And Moon, they are fresh!'

'You say you have rare chops, sir. But I ain't seen nothing but some old defrosted mutton.'

'I've got some of the rarest, thickest and tightest chops you've ever seen.'

'That's some bold chop talk. Care to cook up some chops?'

'Bring it on, fool! First one to miss a note loses.'

He reached for his trumpet case and flicked it open. He pulled out his horn, a dirty bronze mark 3 Geiger, looked like it'd been through a few world wars and in and out of hock for the last fifty years. It was battered and dented and beautiful like the false leg of a woman I once knew. From a side pocket he whipped out his mouthpiece. I tried to see what it was but he'd stuffed it into the valve before I could read it. And then into his fat wet mouth. The only way I was gonna tell if he was playing a Boosey was to get him into the upper registers and listen for the trademark warble.

'What's the tune?' said Bones angrily out of the side of his mouth.

I flicked him a look. 'Blues for Miriam.' He frowned; there was a pause. I smiled.

'You'll pick it up as we go along.' I counted the band in fast.

We started trading fours. Him then me, waiting until someone missed a note. He sizzled all over an F scale like it was his momma's griddle. I folded in a Dorian mode till it was light and fluffy.

We turned the corner on an augmented ninth. Higher and higher I pushed him; I played a fat B minor, and then, there it was, his cheeks expanded and his eyes retracted and slowly but surely out came the beginnings of the high C.

It was at this exact moment that I noticed a couple of ominous cops standing by the bar. Bones saw them too and faltered, the high C he was trying to hold up cracked like a raw egg and leaked all over his face. The band stopped playing, the whole place went quiet. I stepped down off the stage and unscrewed my horn.

'Nice blowing with you. But looks like you got another gig tonight.' I motioned to the cops. 'He's all yours.'

I looked up to say goodbye to Bones but he had a funny look in his eye. But I didn't feel like laughing, it felt all wrong. Then I felt another thing. It was the strong arm of the law tightening around my neck, in stereo.

'Howard Moon?'

'That's me.'

'We are arresting you for the murder of Miriam Pennybaker.'

'Any particular reason?'

'You left this behind.' One of the cops held out a tub of trumpet wax.

'Circumstantial. Anything else?'

'You were seen leaving her apartment this morning.'

'And?'

'And? And your friend Lester Corncrake said you killed her.'

'Right.'

This was not good. Not good at all. It was going to be a long night. What was Lester doing? Who had killed Miriam? Why was Herbie Bones smiling? Why couldn't I breathe? So many questions. The arms continued to squeeze my neck until the room began to darken and spin. I fell to the floor. Herbie Bones stood over me. He unplugged his mouthpiece, the spit from his trumpet dripping on to my shoes.

'Nice chops. Bit overdone,' he said through his smile just before the lights went out. And then I saw it as clear as day inscribed into the rim of his mouthpiece. 'Boosey 1939, Berlin.' I opened my mouth but my throat was blocked by an elephant. One thought passed through my mind, it was definitely time to move out of Stoke Newington . . .

To be continued . . .

Parker man looking through telescope.

Jesus! THIS GUY IS FLANNEL CRAZY.

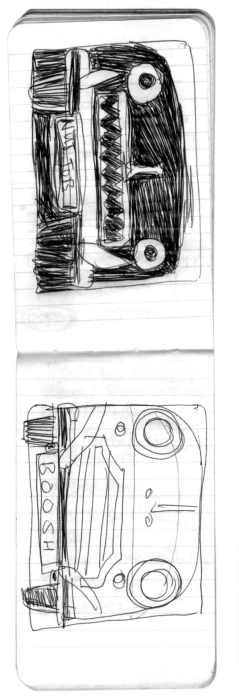

Howard Moon's small book
of poetry
Volume III
The Dairy years

Oh sweet Mrs Gideon,
I stand outside your window in my raincoat
and sing these poems through my hot eyes into
your sleeping mind. Can you hear the music
of my mind raining waxy cream drips across
your large sleeping nose?

Or are you dreaming of another?
If so, ignore these poems.

Oh sweet lady, with your face like a cream oval.
Your nose like a delicious slope of cream.
Your ears like cream flaps.
Your teeth like hard shiny pegs of cream.
Your hair like a hundred brown cream strings.
Your neck, a swooping pedestal of pliable
cream-like material.
Your legs like sturdy bags of hard bendy cream.

Oh sweet Mrs Gideon
Don't let our love go sour like sour cream.

Oh sweet Mrs Gideon,
Your eyes are like two coloured cream balls
swivelling in your creamy sockets.

Your nose like a bulb of cream hanging
sadly twixt two round cream loaves
(or cheekbones).

Your smile is like milk and cream mixed up
with jam and smeared in an upward arc across
your
big white chin.

Your teeth are sixteen long and white pegs
of hardened cream.

Hold my tiny head in your big rough hands and
churn me like curds.

Is it cream that's raining or tears from my tiny
eyes, cream tears, into the cold coffee
of my heart?

Cream **times**

Does cream have a shadow **and if so is it off-white?**

Alternative to cream imagery?

Your delicate **off**-white nose

Your **muffin** legs

Beige hands

Your nutmeg ears **and . . .**

Lovely is your magnolia big toe (good).

The yellowness of the nails only seems to make the whiteness **of your feet all** the brighter as you stroll like a tall horse around the garden.

Through the hedge I see your hair in a fat bun. You look so nice.

Twice I am questioned by police **as I w**rite my poems, **with** my portable typewriter, in the adjacent garden.

Lambo
A DEEPLY EVIL MAN!

June

Nige & Ivana
AKA NIPPLE

Lindsay Christine

A NEW
Tim Hope

SOME
GUY CALLED
SPENCER **ELEANOR** **JAMES DYLAN**

Kingaling

MR & MRS
John Sorapure

When
HARRY MET SALLY

◇ MINDHORN AND THE STOLEN ARMCHAIR ◇

MY NAME IS MINDHORN

BRUNO Mindhorn

I CANNOT MOVE

I HAVE

a trapped NERVE

NO ONE CAN see it though

BECAUSE ITS IN MY LEG

AND now its in your MIND

SEE MY SPECIAL FRIEND

BIRD FRIEND, rescued it

FROM THE Children who CHEWED

HIM, WANTED HIS FEATHERS

INSIDE EM

BUT (YEARS PASSED) NOW WE

SIT

together IN A STOLEN ARMCHAIR

AND HE SINGS to me..

...I HATE WHITES.

...BUY A TRUCK AND RUN MYSELF OVER.

...STOP SNORTING DENTAL FLOSS.

...IS IT BING BING?
OR BING BANG BONG?

...EAT MORE LUMPS.

...BE REALLY NICE TO VINCEY
AND TELL HOWARD TO SHUT UP.

...FIND AT LEAST ONE HUMAN TO
LIKE ME EVERY YEAR.

...ASK BOLLO OUT ON A DATE.

...MOTORCYCLES HAVE TAILS.

...STOP TENNIS RACKETS FROM
FOLLOWING ME INTO THE LOO.

...LEARN HOW TO COOK STEAM.

...HANG OUT AT NABOO'S AND
GET SECONDARY HIGH.

...THROW PARTY FOR ALL
MY NEW TOWELS.

...STOP SAYING THE WORD 'SCHLICKO'

...IS CHEWING EXERCISE?

...CLOTHES ARE NOT OPTIONAL
IN THE TV STORE.

...HAMMOCK TIME!

...WHY?

NABOO'S PLANET

EXT. ALIEN DESERT - EVENING

A BARREN DESERT LANDSCAPE. CAMERA MOVES IN ON A MODEL OF AN ORIENTAL PALACE.

Caption reads . "The other end of the galaxy. 1986."

int. palace - night

A row of pillars lead to a throne upon which sits a king.

A small figure in a cloak walks slowly out of the shadows. We do not see his face.

> KING
> I'm glad you could come.

The figure stops infront of the king.

> KING
> I have summoned you here to the secret chamber. You
> have been chosen from all the people in the kingdom to
> perform a task. it is dangerous but i believe that only you
> could do it. It will be hard and you will almost certainly be
> killed . But if you accept you will be remembered
> throughout history. Do you accept the offer?

The small figure takes off his hood. It is naboo.

> Naboo
> What are the hours ? Do I have to work weekends ?

> KING
> It will take your entire life ...and beyond.

> NABOO
> Well...i haven't got much on. Go on then.

The king stands leads naboo to a bubbling pool of water.

> KING
> This ...is the Jacuzzi of youth.

> NABOO
> The what?

> KING
> i have been it's guardian for many yers. But now i am old
> and my enemies are close.

Hands NABOO a shiney silver cup.

> NABOO
> Whats this ?

1

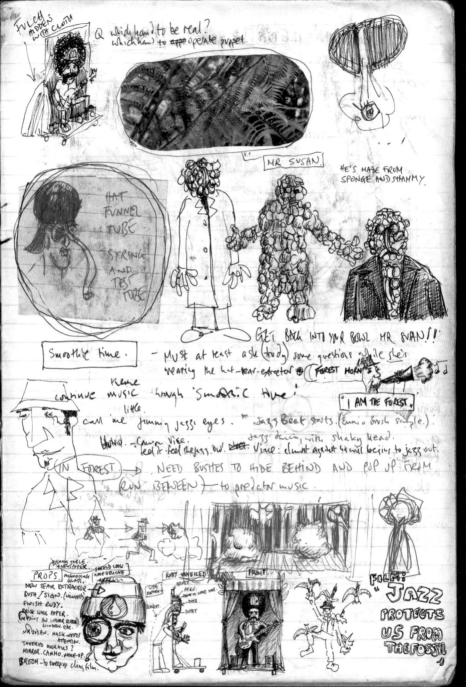

FULCI HIDDEN WITH CLOTH

Q which hand to be real?
which hand to ~~oppo~~ operate puppet.

MR SUSAN

HE'S MADE FROM
SPONGE AND SHAMMY.

HAT
FUNNEL
TUBE

STRING
AND
TEST
TUBE

GET BACK INTO YOUR BOWL MR EVANS!!

Smoothie time.

- MUST at least ask (Trudy) some questions while she's
wearing the hat-~~tear-extractor~~ FOREST HORN

I AM THE FOREST.

Kenne
continue music through 'Smoothie time'
little.
"They call me Jimmy Jazz eyes." Jazz Beat starts. (Ennio Birch sample.)

Jazz dance with shaky head.
Human. - Cameo Vice.
feel it feel the jazz. owl. Vince: element against us will begins to jazz out.

IN FOREST → NEED BUSHES TO HIDE BEHIND AND POP UP FROM
(RUN BETWEEN) — to predator music.

PROPS
NEW TEAR EXTRACTOR
BRUSH / SIGN. (changed)
FINISH RUBY.
BRICK WALL PAPER.
(We build an indoor scene. window. etc.)
MR SUSAN. MASK. NEEDS ATTENTION.
TATTERED OVERALLS?
MIRROR. CAMMO. MAKE-UP.
BROOM — to sweep up cling film.

RUBY UNVEILED   FRONT

FILM: "JAZZ
PROTECTS
US FROM
THE FOSSIL"

ALL FOREST.   ~~QUICK~~   HALF FOREST.

Once upon a time there were two young fellows who lived in a forest. The names were Howard Moon and Vince Noir. ... Howard lived in ... that was a little scary. He had a leaf collection and a ~~trumpet~~ made from an animal horn. ... Vince ...

... star. But he couldn't. He was trapped ... both

... going to get out ...
... Do you know the story ...
Well. There was a mouse and a leopard ... mouse.
~~The mouse was.~~ The mouse was. The ...
The ... big enough. ... slow ... lazy.

BELIEVED BY HIS

... LSE
BUSHES.

... HOOTING IN THE DARKNESS.

... + US BY the camp fire.
... Noel gets scared. ~~Ben~~ wolf dialogue.
... take up off mask — futch. sits down.
... room. for we by the fire." Boys nervous.
... te thing. ~~Feet~~ Howard showing off

◊ MINDHORN'S SONG ◊

MY NAME IS Bruno
MY NAME IS Bruno
I LIVE in THE CORNERS
OF your EYES 
FISHES For breakfast
fishes for tea
IF YOU LOOK INSIDE YOUR KNEES
YOU WILL FIND A FROZEN ME!
MY NAME IS BRUNO
I RIDE A ZEBRA DOWN The SILVER
MINE. THE WINCH-MEN ALL cry
in groups of 3-
"IF YOU LOOK
INSIDE YOUR KNEES
YOU WILL FIND A FROZEN ME!"

HOWARD MOON'S ADVANCED SCHOOL OF ACTING EXPRESSION

POLISH GUILT

CONTEMPLATING GAY

RELIEF OF A MONK

BAKER'S CONFUSION

NORDIC JEALOUSY

GRIEF OF A SAILOR

LUST OF A GARDENER

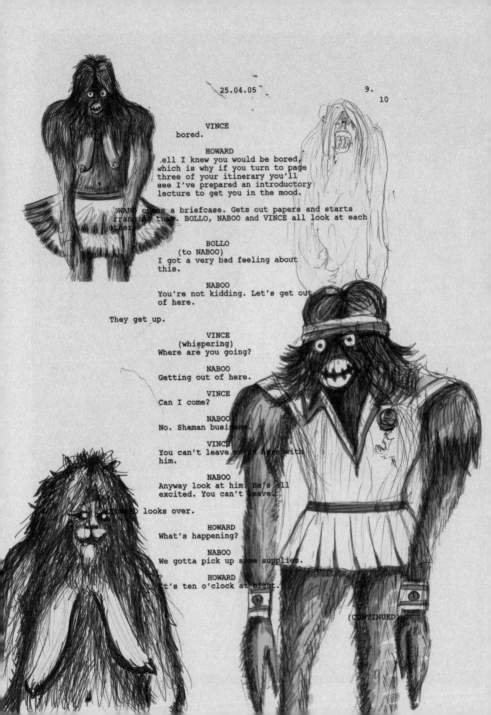

                    VINCE
        bored.

                    HOWARD
        .ell I knew you would be bored,
        which is why if you turn to page
        three of your itinerary you'll
        see I've prepared an introductory
        lecture to get you in the mood.

)WARD opens a briefcase. Gets out papers and starts
        rranging them. BOLLO, NABOO and VINCE all look at each
        other.

                    BOLLO
                (to NABOO)
        I got a very bad feeling about
        this.

                    NABOO
        You're not kidding. Let's get out
        of here.

        They get up.

                    VINCE
                (whispering)
        Where are you going?

                    NABOO
        Getting out of here.

                    VINCE
        Can I come?

                    NABOO
        No. Shaman business.

                    VINCE
        You can't leave me in here with
        him.

                    NABOO
        Anyway look at him. He's all
        excited. You can't leave.

)WARD looks over.

                    HOWARD
        What's happening?

                    NABOO
        We gotta pick up some supplies.

                    HOWARD
        t's ten o'clock at night.

                                    (CONTINUED)

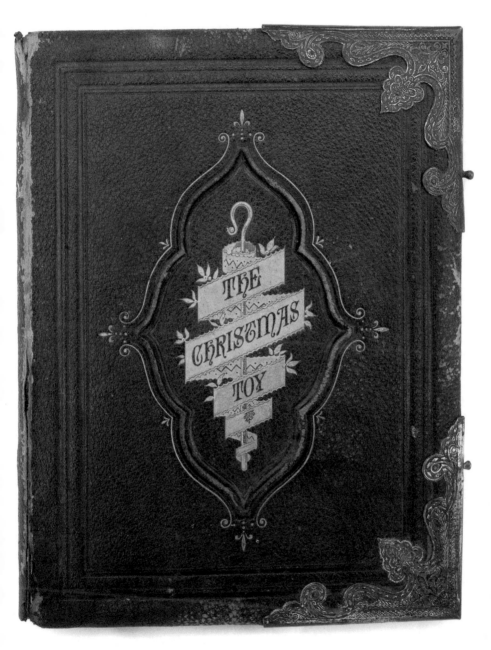

THE CHRISTMAS TOY

CHRISTMAS TOY

A story by Vince Noir

Dedicated to all the indie boys across the land who like to wear the occasional eyeliner or tight trouser.

Once upon a time, on a snowy winter's evening, Christmas Toy was skipping through the Enchanted Wood when he saw a warm orange light off in the distance through a clearing in the trees. The fiery beacon seemed to be drawing him in like a powerful yellow magnet. Christmas Toy raced towards the flame, almost in a trance. Five minutes later he found himself on Kentish Town High Street, on the borders of Camden market, standing outside a huge inn that was bristling with life and strange energy. Christmas Toy, barely a man himself, could not open the huge wooden door on his own and had to sit patiently for some real people to come along to the inn so he could scuttle in behind them with legs like two rulers.

Once inside, Christmas Toy looked around all the people inside and smi and saw in the corner of the room a log fire dancing on the floor. He jum up and down with excitement, open his new surroundings.

It was about this point that a group of thick-necked tattooed yo-yos saw Christmas Toy dancing in front of th fire enjoying himself thoroughly.

'Look at that litter bug!' said yo-yo No. 1.

'What a nonce bag!' agreed yo-yo No.2, spitting out beer pork scratchings in disgust.

'Look at his outfit!' snarled yo-yo No. 3.
'It's a little girl's one.'

All the yo-yos laughed together lik pack of wild dogs. The laughter turn into table banging and then finally a animalistic howl. Christmas Toy wa little taken aback but thought to hims *'They can't be laughing at my little r soldier's top? I got this from Top Sh in the girls' section.*

It was quite expensive. Must be some kind of private joke between one yo-yo and another. Yo-yo humour, I expect.'

Christmas Toy smiled and thanked the fire for the dancing, skipped off to the bar leaving a trail of glitter behind him.

Half an hour later Christmas Toy had been lifted on to the tall bar stool by two Camden girls called Josie and Carla. The three of them were chatting away and trying quite a lot of fizzy blue champagne. You see, Christmas Toy had been the best-selling toy that year and the royalties had come flooding in.

'Drinks on me!' he shouted, as more and more people gathered around: girls, boys, boys who looked like girls, and even the landlord of the inn, who had mod glasses and legs like Pan.

Christmas Toy seemed to be the centre of attention and was loving every minute of it. Yo-yo No. 1 stared over in disbelief and said,
'Look at that creepy little twat acting like it's his birthday.'
Yo-yo No. 2 growled,
'It'll be his deathday soon if he doesn't watch out.'

Yo-yo No. 3 agreed and ordered another bucket of scratchings.

Christmas Toy was having a brilliant time, and felt shiny and special. Everyone tried to give the toy free clothes and strange magic beans that made his head spin round and round and his eyes seem even bigger than usual. One man loved the Christmas Toy so much he gave him a whole handful of magic beans, silver and green, then filmed the toy accepting them on his mobile phone. *'Ahh, it's nice to have a souvenir,'* the Toy thought. The man quickly left and hailed a taxi to Fleet Street.

As the night wore on Christmas Toy was dancing on air (literally, it was a trick he'd picked up in the Enchanted Wood). He seemed to have over a thousand friends now and offers of film scripts, photoshoots, voiceovers, free television sets. He couldn't believe it, everyone was so kind and friendly and nice in Kentish Town.

The yo-yos stared on at Christmas Toy in a sinister way.

'Who does he think he is? The Mayor of Camden?'
yo-yo No. 1 said sarcastically.

'Actually I think he might be,'
yo-yo No. 2 said.

'Isn't that your girlfriend he's talking to?'
enquired yo-yo No. 3.

'Right, that is it! HE'S WELL DEAD!!'
screamed yo-yo No.4.

The yo-yos charged the Christmas Toy like a pack of wild boars and pulverised his tiny frame with bar stools and glasses and pink sausagey fists. The Christmas Toy was sprawled around the sticky pub floor with arms and legs everywhere.

'That'll teach you to be on digital telly,'
said yo-yo No. 1.

'Yeah, you knob'ead,'
yo-yo No. 2 piped up.

'You might want to think twice about wearing eyeliner, you transsexual rapist,'
yo-yo No. 3 said, spitting on the ground near Christmas Toy's decapitated head.

The yo-yos marched out of the inn into the starry Camden night in search of slowly rotating soft greymeat. The Toy had double vision and internal bleeding and was staring at a vomit

stain on the ceiling of the inn, wondering
how someone had managed to fire
it up that high. He lay on the floor for
what seemed like an eternity.
Finally, a woman appeared above him,
like a mirage in the desert.

'At last,' Christmas Toy thought,
*'a kind lady's here to put me back
together and offer me cab money home.'*

   The woman bent down and shouted,
*'How dare you use Myface to try and
get my daughter's mobile phone number,
you evil toy! She's only twelve!
What are you? A paedophile?'*

   *'Er, but I don't even have a Myface.
I can't work computers!'*
the Toy pleaded.

'Whatever,'
the vexed lady whispered, and gathered
up Christmas Toy's stray limbs,
throwing them into the murky dark
green waters of Camden canal.

   Christmas Toy, now just a torso,
rolled back to the Enchanted Forest
under the ultraviolet bridge, through
piles of crunchy leaves, dead pigeons
and needles. He thought to himself that
maybe being one of the biggest-selling
toys of the year wasn't all it was
cracked up to be really.

The End

Betamax

The black rider.
An obsolete
format bitter and
enraged, Enemy of
V·H·S

A kind of evil
Zorro made from
tapes with one
central eye.
and tape arms
ready to lassoo
★ in anyone
he chooses.

The Western Town

◊ MINDHORN'S ESTRANGED HORSE ◊

I AWOKE THIS MORNING
AND SMASHED MY WAY
INTO THE BATHROOM WINDOW
TO FIND
MY WEARY WIFE
ASLEEP IN THE LEGS OF
HORACE MY (ESTRANGED) HORSE.
QUITE ENTRANCED I REMOVED HER
CHANDELIER, DUSTED THE PIECES,
CONSUMED ALL BUT TWO
AND HAVE NOW AT LEISURE
DEPARTED FOR BRUGES.
MINDHORN, BRUNO

HAMILTON CORK

IT IS SAID THAT AWARD WINNING AND CRITICALLY ACCLAIMED AUTHOR AND PUBLISHER HAMILTON CORK HAS THE ABILITY TO DETERMINE A BOOK'S QUALITY AND POTENTIAL SIMPLY BY READING THE FIRST SENTENCE. THE FOLLOWING SENTENCES ARE SOME OF HAMILTON'S PERSONAL FAVOURITES.

The shed pulsated and glided along the street consuming rubbish and stray cats like a wooden basking shark.

I threw myself on to Jesus and crushed him flat with my boomerangs.

Chi and Ricard tied their hair together, loaded their pistols and began to boogie to the hot Latin beats.

Underwater Steve went crazy when he was photographed.

I was seven years old when I realised I had the ability to eat other people's shadows.

The pirates all looked at the plate of freshly cut sandwiches before them and immediately burst into tears.

George and Steve were identical in every way – they had soft blonde hair on their eyes and matching metallic ballbags.

Although she wouldn't admit it, Jill knew she was slowly turning into a hula hoop.

Throughout history I have presented myself as a series of patterns.

Cats, cats, cats, everywhere cats, but then, stepping out from the crowd, a single crab.

It was Wednesday today, which was strange as yesterday was Friday.

Zoobrella was her name and she shone like a fresh crystal chrysanthemum from sector 5G.

Cancel the cakes, Marjorie, Sebastian's gonna use a trenchcoat instead.

Ian cried tears on to the hard shell of the dead crab and knew in his heart he was finally a man.

An eyeball as big as a car and fingers like summer hosepipes: this guy wasn't fucking around!

Old Freeman catalogues and a dead kangaroo were all Steve could think about.

Love was something for other people – Mungo had tried once but it made him feel like a silly sausage.

Tex stood at the back of the room in his enormous yellow trousers, hoping and wondering.

The whole room had steamed up with hot baby breath, the tennis had started again and Sebastian was furious!

Ian wrestled the worm for sixteen hours, stopping only once for a bowl of Ricicles.

The bass guitar slid down the back of the chair and connected with the front teeth of the piano: both instruments looked embarrassed.

THE VELVET ONION PRESENTS

VINCE NOIR'S ELECTRO CIRCUS

❧ PROUD TO PRESENT A SENSATIONAL NIGHT of CABARET ❧

FEATURING

EXCLUSIVE LIVE PERFORMANCES FROM

SAMMY THE CRAB
BAMBOO FORK
THE GREAT SANTINI

THE BLUE McENROES
THE UMPIRE OF FOLK
THE BLACK TUBES

𝔞𝔫𝔡 MANY MORE

The Priest and the beast (Spider Dijon and Rudy Van Disarzio)

"What men do for those one and a half minutes of pleasure makes a mockery of civilisation."

MUTANT QUESTIONS ABOUT THE OUTSIDE WORLD

Having been the subject of Dixon Bainbridge's hideously gruesome experiments in the 1950s in which animals are mutated with different body parts, Howard and Vince break into the lab to set them free. When they open the cage and offer them their freedom, however, the Mutants are so used to their lifestyle in captivity, that they question the very meaning of freedom. *'What is freedom?'* asks the head and perhaps most disgusting-looking Mutant.

This is Howard's response, which has to go down as one of the most eloquent speeches of all time . . . yeah right!:

Howard: *'Freedom is a place, a place where you can dream. A place where you can run. A place without walls, without boundaries, without –'*

Mutant: *'Cups? Are there cups?'*

The viewer never gets to hear all of the other questions the Mutants have. Here is just a small snippet of their queries:

IS THERE BACON?

DO PEOPLE STILL
OWN ROCKETS?

WON'T I BE KILLED
BY AIR?

MAY I STEAL AN EGG
FROM YOUR GARDEN?

WILL THERE BE LARGE
BREASTED CHAIRS?

CAN I BURY
A KNITTED CAN?

WILL I WEEP?

DO SANDWICHES STILL
COST 12,000 POUNDS?

HOW DO I TELL
PEOPLE ABOUT MY
TENDENCY TO LEAK?

ARE THERE
SNOW BOMBS
IN THE LAKE?

DOES SOUND
STILL MAKE
NOISE?

WHY DO MY
EYES STINK?

ARE YOU ROTTING
TOO?

WHO DO
I SPEAK
TO ABOUT
WALKING?

HOW MUCH
MUD SHOULD I
TAKE FOR

MY JOURNEY?

DOES DOUG STILL RUN
THE SHOP BY THE CHERRY
DONUT PLACE NEXT TO
THE THING?

WHERE DO CAKES
TAKE A NAP?

HOW WILL I SAND
MY BASKETS?

MAY I DRIVE NAKED?

MAY I CRY ON YOUR TOES?

MAY I TURN SLIGHTLY
SO THAT MY ANUS CAN
SEE YOU?

DO YOU STILL MILK MY LAWN?

WHERE ARE THE
CHOPPING PEOPLE?

I SPILT SOMETHING
CAN I SELL IT?

WHEN DO I SMELL?
DO CARS STILL RULE THE
WIZARD SECTOR?

MAY I BEAT UP YOUR
SINK TONIGHT?

CAN I GET A JOB AS
A ROASTED PEANUT?

WILL THE AIR FORCE
TOUCH ME?

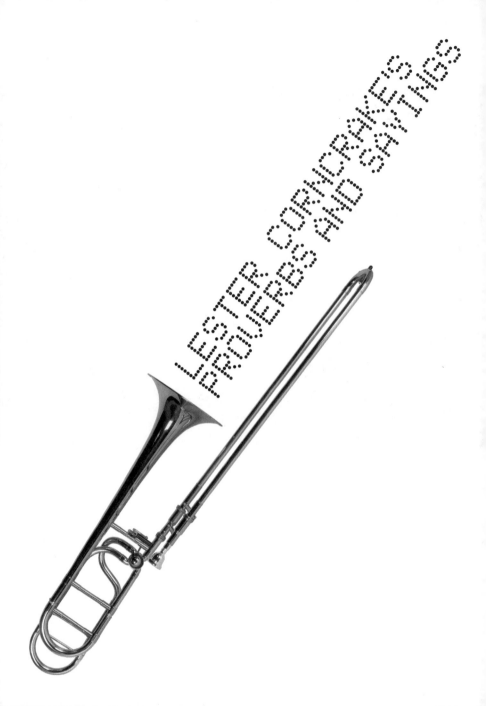

- Every journey begins with a giant shit.

- If you ever get nervous before a gig, just imagine that the audience is covered in maggots (if I imagine that they're in their pants, I get too **horn**y).

- Women **love men wit**h boobies.

- Practice don't mean diddly unless you practise at it.

- Always eat a gallon of ice cream **15 mi**nutes before a gig and a ha**nd**ful of sauce (any kind **will do**). It takes your mind off playing cuz you're too busy puking.

- Never sleep with a man's wife . . . unless she **really wa**nts to do it.

- I loooo**ooooo**ove to go through people's wallets.

- I'd rather **be** blind than see with **no wisdom** . . . Wait, fuck that, I'll take the sight.

- It's not **whether yo**u **win or lose**, it's whether Lead Lips Re**dbe**lly gives me my godd**amn flug**elhorn back!

- Music soothes the savage beast and that's really cool cuz those beasts are **m**ean muthafuckers.

- Love is like a clarinet. It's long and bl**ack and o**nce you p**lay it, you** move on to the oboe.

- Never make love to **an animal** you never met.

- When I **wa**s in World War II . . . **That**'s it.

- Despite all of **ou**r **differences** in the human race, people really are different.

- The best way to tell if someone's good in **be**d i**s** the way they **eat a bowl** of gravy.

◇ MINDHORN AND MRS CHINA ◇

My name is <u>MINDHORN</u>
I swim backwards
         FORWARDS
                S
                I
                D
                E
                  WAYS.
I'm in love with a woman,
shes got no EYES.
    I found her drawing cows
near BRUGES.
I DONT KNOW HER name
SO I CALL HER
         Mrs China. She
were a coiffeur but
IT ENDED IN BLOODSHED.
Now she lives in a glass case
    IN THE TOWNHALL IN GHENT
and every 3 YEARS
    (on a tuesday)
    I DUST

        <u>HER</u>

ANIMAL
OFFENDERS
MOST WANTED

DERRICK
THE RACIST OCELOT

This guy is real bad. There is no animal he doesn't hate. He once Called a squirrel a Nut Retard seven times from the back seat of a Lincoln. Currently serving 3 days for telling a homeless Elk to get a job.

CARL
THE VANDALISING JACK RABBIT

Ooh, this guy can mess shit up. He once overturned 18 skips in less than 2 minutes, with one leg! He also throws eggs at funerals for dead plants. Currently doing community service cleaning up a swamp that he filled with syrup.

SHEILA
THE LIZARD
WHO PARKS IN
HANDICAPPED SPOTS

This lady lizard is off her crock. She doesn't have any physical problems yet she insists on parking in the handicapped spot. One time, she cut off a one-legged millipede to get the spot. now that's pure liquid evil! Currently serving hard time at the Swansea Driving Academy.

GEORGE
THE MACKEREL THAT
EXPOSES HIMSELF

This George guy is a real pervert. He once showed his whole fin to a school of Sunfish... in the middle of the day even! He never learns his lesson, either. He's been arrested for public exposure over 3,000 times. More people have seen this guy's gills than their own feet. He's also known for keeping bad company: his childhood friends include Tommy, the Rapist Crab, and Emerson, the Masturbating Whale.

JERRY
THE DRUG
DEALING DINGO

This one is into some bad trouble. He's the number one dealer in Australia and usually transports his stash in the pouches of his marsupial friends. One time, he didn't even tell Boris, the Duck-Billed Platypus, that he put 40 kilos of acid in his duodenum. Not a nice guy.

ANIMAL OFFENDERS

MOST WANTED CONT.

WANDA
THE SWAN THAT KEYS CARS

This swan won't just settle for floating on a lake and looking at her reflection. no, Wanda likes to key any car she can find and they don't even have to be parked! ever since her dad got squashe by a Hyundai, she's been on a crazy car key rampage.

HERSCHEL
THE BABOON THAT WALKS INTO LIFTS AND PRESSES ALL THE FLOORS

This guy is a lot worse than he sounds. Imagine being late for a meeting because some 500-pound baboon with a red ass ru in and presses all the buttons – what a not nice jerk! Herschel i also known for lighting his own poop and ringing doorbells and selling life insurance.

What follows is an extract from the film criticism of Jurgen Harbourmaster (*The Doctor and the Pencil*), one of the most controversial and, ultimately, lonely filmmakers around. Harbourmaster has so keenly guarded his independence that, until this article was published recently in *Behind Flicks*, he insisted that all his writing be buried in forests, so as to avoid censorship or 'human contamination'.

'**Critic** *krit'ik,* **n.** one skilled in estimating the quality of literary or artistic work: a professional reviewer: one skilled in textual studies, various readings, and the ascertainment of the original words: a fault-finder.'

Fault-finder? This pompous crap is why I rarely refer to dictionaries. (The one from which the above definition came now lies in tatters on the bare stone floor of my studio, covered in hate. I have since resolved to ignore any words I don't already know). I am a celebrater (is this a word?). A champion. I write film criticism because I'm in love with cinema. All right! Stop shouting at me. I know she's been unfaithful, producing numerous bloated and festeringly pornographic bastard offspring (notably James Cameron; who can sit through *Titanic* without attempting suicide at least once?). But I'm a romantic. Ever since I snuck into an underground showing of *Drill Crazy* (half skin–flick, half Black and Decker commercial), my mind has been wedged open with her wonder. Which is why the hobbling puke that cinema has become rankles so much in my Viking belly.

I took my godson Fritz to see *The Exorcist* so that we could both mock its cosy, bourgeois banality. But because of the archaic rules of classification, and because he is three years old, the cinema manager wouldn't let us in. I pleaded with the name-tagged buffoon, and made enough idle threats for him to say he'd radio for help if I didn't 'get a hold of myself'. Faced with dumping the child in the foyer or missing the film, I ended up having to sneak the thankless beast into the screening in my duffel bag. After shaking him, the boy's cardio-vascular system spluttered back into life just in time for him to catch the film's opening. His face was a picture. He screamed so loud that his face looked like latex stretched over a coat-hanger.

Fritz's mother told me that the boy is no longer able to sleep. Good. No one needs to sleep for fifteen hours a day. He was obviously complacent. I sleep one hour a week. I watch films. I write films. I make films. I exist. Remember: all a man needs to live is:

1. An ashtray.
2. Some food.
Oh, and something called celluloid.

Ok. Now, ladies, eyes down looking, here we go:

Doggy doo, Number 62

Two bloody stumps, Number 11

My mind is filled with goo, Number 32

The age I lost my virginity, Number 43
That's right, Number 43 Lucky me!

The right side of my face is feeling numb, Number 31

Howdy doody bouncing clown, Number 75

Fee Fi Foo, Number 32

Uuuuuuuuuummmmmm, Number 84

On its own, Number 64

No pets go to heaven, Number 27

After 7 heart attacks, I can't believe I'm
still alive, Number 105

The year I learned to walk, Number 12

Right now I have no pants on, Number 28

My father's a male whore, Number 204

My wife says I have no spine, Number 39

All the fours, Number 10

I just sniffed some furniture glue, Number 172

I do graffiti just for kicks, Number 86

The number of fingers on a hand missing
two fingers, Number 3

I have to take a massive pee, Number 33

I just bought a Kazoo, Number 202

My collection of pen flutes fell off a cliff in Devon,
Number 97

Beelzebub, Lucifer, the Devil himself,
all the 6s, Number 666 . . .

IDEAS FOR EDINBURGH

RAP LITTLE DEER SONG

- Tommy
- Deer song
- Morgan
- Rox idea's
- Delivery Man
- Old lady
- Puppet Man
- Telephone
- Ramslegs
- Monkey Carol

• Jeff
  Wildlife Conservation

• Bent wolves • Klause

Married on the moron

Julian as a fair lady amongst the
Brazon.

RAMSLEGS

Bin Bags running away.
↓
Short films

Punching and kissing alternatively

A PUPPET MAN

Coming at ya
like a muffin

↕

TELEPHONE MESSAGES

Top headed Man

Goo her two one of the tops.

(Man covered in tops who is chased out of the theatre
he always comes back and sticks food to his hair tops)

Jack Frost and his freezer Bag.

Jack Frost comes in with a huge
freezer bag and there is SFX
of a blizzard or snow storm
everyone freezes and
Jack gets out
lollipop and
puts them
on everyone.

Or gives. Some to audience
he leaves and the show
continues.

large orange
Monster
who sings
JAZZ

then gets
ejected.

BENT WOLVES

Uncle Wolf Nightmare J
Julian pulling himself along
on a trolly covered in a
blanket to music.

Drum e Bass
Jungle Cobra.

THE MOUTH OF SHADOWS

Foam
Fire

Horn   mirror

Toney's Manta Ray poem

Timothy eyes of the Ray

BENT WOLVES

Noel e Julian Run on in painted
wooden masks of wolves faces wearing
fur coats. They Dance or play chess
or just do strange acrobatics then leave
again   maybe 3 times in the show.

Band Stuff

V: I'M in a Band

H: Oh yeah

V: The onion stealer

H: Never heard of them

V: You will be, we've all got quiffs

M: What type of music is it?

H: I Dont   I'm not really interested in that side of things.

I Dont   Sing about BROOMS
I Sing about love.

MR SUSAN A MAN MADE ENTIRELY OF FRUIT.

Get back in your band
you freak!

Howard: I've brought in MR
SUSAN

◊ MINDHORN AND THE DEAD LADY OF CALAIS ◊

MY NAME IS MINDHORN

Bruno Mindhorn
STANDING IN MY
TOWER by the AUTOBAHN
SELLING MOTHS
by the OUNCE
to The Strangers
I KEEP THEM IN MY WIG
AND WEIGH THEM HOURLY

BRUNO HASNT SOLD A MOTH IN MONTHS, NOT
A WING
EXCEPT To a DEA~~R~~D 
LADY OF CALAIS. I EXCHANGED
ONE FOR HER WOODEN TRAY THEN
SHE DROVE AWAY.

B. MINDHORN

O₀ O₀ O₀

I DID A TWISTY

O₀ O₀ O₀

A TINY TWISTY

TWIST HIM UP

TWIST HIM DOWN

TWIST HIM ALL AROUND

LIKE THE COBRA

DANCING TO THE MUSIC OF

THE PIPE, THE PIPE, THE PIPE

THE PIPE OF LIFE

A₀ E E AI E E AH EE AI

KALAMAR SHALAMAR

CINEMA IN THE NIGHT

IT'S SUCH A GOOD THING

DON'T FORGET TO BRING

POPCORN TONY AND HIS

PAPER CASTLE

THE MIGHTY BOOSH: LIVE 2008/9

SEPTEMBER
11 EDINBURGH FESTIVAL THEATRE
12 EDINBURGH FESTIVAL THEATRE
13 GLASGOW PAVILION
14 GLASGOW PAVILION
16 DUBLIN OLYMPIA
18 DUBLIN OLYMPIA
19 DUBLIN OLYMPIA
20 DUBLIN OLYMPIA
22 YORK OPERA HOUSE
23 YORK OPERA HOUSE
24 YORK OPERA HOUSE
25 YORK OPERA HOUSE
26 HARROGATE THEATRE
27 HARROGATE THEATRE
29 HUDDERSFIELD LAWRENCE BATLEY
30 HUDDERSFIELD LAWRENCE BATLEY

OCTOBER
01 BUXTON OPERA HOUSE
02 BUXTON OPERA HOUSE
03 WAKEFIELD THEATRE ROYAL
04 WAKEFIELD THEATRE ROYAL
06 SHEFFIELD CITY HALL
07 SHEFFIELD CITY HALL
08 SHEFFIELD CITY HALL
09 SHEFFIELD CITY HALL
11 SHEFFIELD CITY HALL
14 LIVERPOOL ARENA
15 LIVERPOOL ARENA
16 BLACKPOOL OPERA HOUSE
17 BLACKPOOL OPERA HOUSE
18 CARDIFF CIA
20 LONDON BRIXTON ACADEMY
21 LONDON BRIXTON ACADEMY
22 LONDON BRIXTON ACADEMY
23 LONDON BRIXTON ACADEMY
24 LONDON BRIXTON ACADEMY
25 LONDON BRIXTON ACADEMY
27 BRISTOL HIPPODROME
28 BRISTOL HIPPODROME
29 BRISTOL HIPPODROME
30 BRISTOL HIPPODROME
31 BIRMINGHAM NIA

NOVEMBER
01 BIRMINGHAM NIA
03 OXFORD NEW THEATRE
04 OXFORD NEW THEATRE
05 WOLVERHAMPTON CIVIC
06 WOLVERHAMPTON CIVIC
07 NOTTINGHAM ARENA
08 NOTTINGHAM ARENA
10 PORTSMOUTH GUILDHALL
11 PORTSMOUTH GUILDHALL
12 BRIGHTON CENTRE
13 BRIGHTON CENTRE
14 BRIGHTON CENTRE
15 BRIGHTON CENTRE
17 PLYMOUTH PAVILIONS
18 PLYMOUTH PAVILIONS
19 BOURNEMOUTH BIC
21 BOURNEMOUTH BIC
22 BOURNEMOUTH BIC
24 CARDIFF CIA
26 NEWCASTLE ARENA
27 NEWCASTLE ARENA
28 GLASGOW SECC
29 GLASGOW SECC

DECEMBER
01 MANCHESTER APOLLO
02 MANCHESTER APOLLO
03 MANCHESTER APOLLO
04 MANCHESTER APOLLO
05 MANCHESTER MEN ARENA
06 MANCHESTER MEN ARENA
08 LEEDS GRAND
09 LEEDS GRAND
10 LEEDS GRAND
11 LEEDS GRAND
12 LONDON WEMBLEY ARENA
13 BRIGHTON CENTRE
15 LONDON WEMBLEY ARENA
17 LONDON O2
22 BIRMINGHAM NIA
23 MANCHESTER MEN ARENA

JANUARY
07 SHEFFIELD ARENA
10 NOTTINGHAM ARENA
14 GLASGOW SECC
16 ABERDEEN AECC
17 ABERDEEN AECC

ON TOUR

IN DA FUTURE

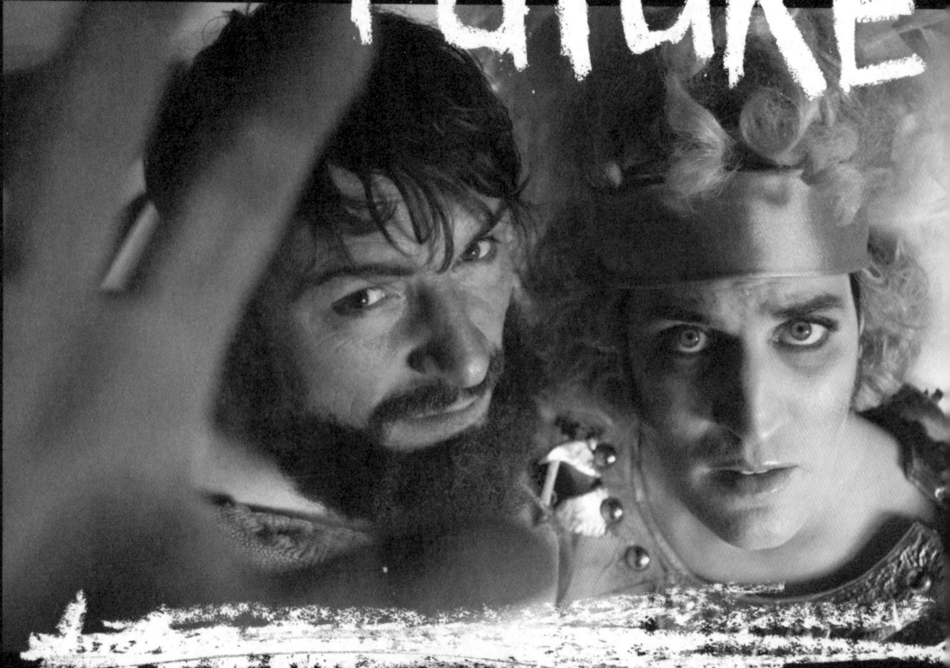

CHARLIE & THE BLACK N WHITE RAINBOW

As Charlie tumbled into view like a pink mountain in a model village, his attention was drawn towards a freaky Black n White Rainbow who seemed to be imprisoned in some kind of bamboo crate.

The Black n White Rainbow was screaming the way a half-boiled empty kettle does. Charlie couldn't stand the noise and threw a yellow sandal at the idiot stranger. 'Why would you make a noise like that?' Charlie enquired, still slightly vexed.

The Black n White Rainbow produced a beautiful blonde guitar and began to tell his sad tale. The Rainbow's voice (now calmer) was chilling and reminiscent of Joan Baez. He explained that racists had beaten him senseless and finally locked him up while they went gambling at Wimbledon dog track.

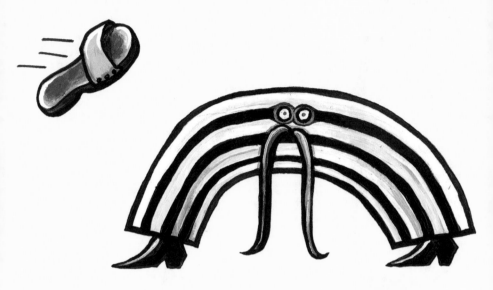

Charlie had no reason to doubt the Black n White Rainbow and immediately picked the lock with an antique hatpin. Now free, the Black n White Rainbow seemed unhinged and slightly berserk. He danced around in a frenzy, rolled in the dirt and pumped invisible lovers the way a madman or a rapist would.

Charlie became nervous and started to back away. The Black n White Rainbow shouted out some swear words and began eating loose dog shit off the floor. Now terrified, Charlie hailed a black taxi cab and tried to put as much distance between himself and the Black n White Rainbow as possible.

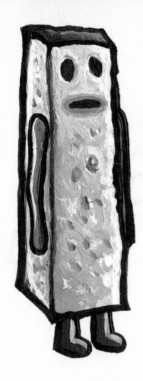

Charlie went to bed that night knowing in his heart he had unleashed a demon, possibly the Devil himself. He hoped the Rainbow would calm down, maybe get a job in a photocopy centre, take a wife and buy a place in Highgate village.

The next morning Charlie woke up at noon and prepared his usual breakfast (15 boiled eggs and a policeman's helmet full of muesli). As he was dipping soft bread soldiers Into the golden yolk his heart nearly burst through his pink chest. It wasn't the food that caused this reaction but the small voice coming from within the digital radio Charlie had tuned to 'Planet Rock'.

Charlie made strange faces and winced as the 'news flash' danced in front of him and wee'd on his back (metaphorically). It seemed that after Charlie had taken his taxi the Black n White Rainbow became even more insane, stomping around town in Chelsea boots causing untold mayhem.

A LIST OF THE MAYHEM

(Crimes the Rainbow performed in no particular order):

1. Left used needles in the Brownies' clubhouse.

2. Poked an Indian boy in the eye with his see-through winky tube.

3. Raped a designer coat.

4. Burnt down the Hawley Arms.

5. Gathered up an army of scarecrows and took them to a nursery, mentally scarring the toddlers.

6. Drew a picture of Peter Kay on a cornish pasty and threw it into a maze.

7. Hurt Alan Sugar's wife with a big lolly.

8. Pretended to be Welsh.

There was no number 9.

The Rainbow not only murdered, raped and mocked the innocent but his behaviour had an unusual side-effect. Every time the arch-shaped character was successfully evil a small amount of colour drained from his surroundings and into his own black n white format (highly unusual).

He had been up all night working like a freelance scientist, so as a result virtually all the colours from life had been sucked deep inside him. He was no longer black n white but life around him had become so. (A motherfucking reversal.)

A black n white world was no good to anyone. Flowers seemed pointless, great masterpieces became colouring books, and snooker was virtually impossible. (Jimmy White cried for over forty minutes.)

Charlie knew he had to do something, the world was in a black n white funk and it was up to him to save the day. The problem was that the more colour the Rainbow sucked from life the more powerful he became. Colour was like crack cocaine to the Rainbow and he sucked it through a glass pipe straight into his bloodstream.

Charlie knew he had to stop the rainbow but the question was 'how?' Charlie wasn't very fast, he was pretty unfit in general. He played five-a-side football occasionally but was teased by his friends who called him the 'Pink Jan Mølby'. He could spray the ball around nicely but his movement was minimal.

Also, Charlie was terrible at fighting. He once got beaten up by a large otter called Steve Bendelack, who kicked him to the floor, stood on his face and proceeded to throw his hat into the river and use it as a neat black ferry.

Charlie knew he would have to 'box clever'. He enlisted the help of Columbo, the LA cop in the crumpled mac, who had the appearance of a tatty moth but was actually as sharp as homemade lemonade.

Columbo's first idea was to find out where the Rainbow lived, wait for him to go out and then snoop about in his dwellings, looking for any weak spots or points of interest. It turned out that the Rainbow lived in a canvas tent inside Battersea Power Station.

Charlie and Columbo parked across the street from the brown eyesore and waited for the rainbow to appear. Eventually the evil Rainbow (now almost neon in colour and vibrating) leapt through the door with the strength of a powerful flea and disappeared up the road in the direction of Clapham, with only one thing on his mind: crimes.

Charlie and Columbo left it five minutes, then put down their doughnuts and coffee and entered one of the most ugly but interesting buildings ever to grace the London skyline.

Once inside they found exactly what they were looking for. The place was a tip and amongst the rubbish were several dildos and empty KFC boxes. But Columbo quickly homed in on the Rainbow's record collection. Nothing but Bob Dylan records. He had everything, from the *Basement Tapes* to *Blood on the Tracks*.

The Rainbow was clearly obsessed. Columbo realised that if they were going to catch the multicoloured nut job they would have to enlist the help of Bob Dylan. Maybe organise a gig and lure the Rainbow in, trap him, and take back all the colour he had stolen from the rest of the world.

Once the situation was explained to Bob he was more than happy to help and the day of the concert came around quickly.

Charlie positioned himself adjacent to the stage, disguised as a hot dog vendor. Columbo dressed up as a roadie and hovered in the wings, head-to-foot in denim.

C.S.S. played first, then Mad Timmy the Talking Sandcastle, who did a tight racist five. Then followed a short interval. Eventually the moment everyone was waiting for: Dylan took to the stage. He launched into an obscure cover version of 'Girl You Know It's True' by Milli Vanilli (the pretty boy fuckwits who fooled the world by miming an entire album). Bob then tried a harmonica version of a Tangerine Dream song, but there was still no sign of the demented slice of colours.

Finally Bob played a few songs from Desire and the crime lord appeared as if by magic (well, in a golf cart). The crowd had been instructed to block the Rainbow's view and Charlie further taunted him by pelting hot dogs at his red and green temples. The Rainbow began moshing violently and started to foam at the mouth.

Columbo tampered with the sound, causing a high-pitched wail to emanate from Bob's guitar, particularly painful for coloured prisms of light, and dogs. The Rainbow's ears began to bleed and Mongo (the local butcher's dog) had a series of small heart attacks. The Rainbow staggered forward to the front of the stage, punching small indie girls in the face. Nothing was going to stop him enjoying his favourite song, 'Picnic At Bear Mountain Massacre Blues'.

As he lunged at the trendies the crowd suddenly parted and the Rainbow disappeared into a deep hole just in front of the photographers' pit. Knowing the game was up, the Rainbow screamed up to the heavens the way Robert Mitchum does in The Night of the Hunter (sadly the only film Charles Laughton ever directed) and began stamping his feet through the floor like a bigger, more colourful Rumpelstiltskin.

Bob finished the gig and the crowd cheered and slowly left for the last tube. As people were leaving, Charlie swears he heard two fans say that although Dylan was magical, things were just not the same since everything had turned black n white in the world.

A vet was promptly called and the mad Rainbow was shot in the face with a powerful horse tranquilliser called Regretamin. Once the Rainbow fell unconscious, Charlie, Columbo and the vet jumped into the pit and began extracting colour from him and squirting it back into life.

It was a slow process and after an hour and a half they all stopped for hot dogs and tea from white polystyrene cups. Bob didn't physically help, but he did crouch at the side of the hole and shout instructions to the others, telling them where they were going wrong.

They worked into the night and eventually all the colour was drained from the Rainbow and put back into life, all except a small amount that Charlie had spilled in his tea and accidentally drunk by mistake, which meant that the whole Universe was returned back to its usual vibrant colour, all apart from one shoe that the vet was wearing.

Bob took a shine to the only remaining black n white object and said he would like to keep it as a souvenir and even waived his fee in exchange for it.

The next day the Rainbow awoke from his K-hole coma. He felt weak and colourless, a sharp contrast to the world around him, which was now bright and causing his rods and cones to go apeshit. He slipped on a pair of sunglasses he had stolen from Ricardo Tubbs in the 80s and wondered what his next move would be.

At this point Charlie appeared and shouted down to the Rainbow that although no charges were to be brought against him, he should definitely have a long, hard look at himself. The Rainbow apologised and explained that he was slightly insane due to a traumatic childhood.

Charlie again felt sorry for the Rainbow and lowered a rope ladder down into the hole. The Rainbow climbed to freedom and shuffled around, staring at his feet and mumbling about all the trouble he had caused everyone. He said that although fairly abstract it was still wrong to steal colour from the Universe.

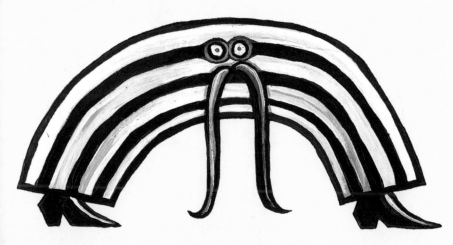

Charlie gave the Rainbow a full-length mirror and said that if he ever felt like committing such crimes again he should look into his own reflection and the reflection of his eyes, and there he would see love.

Charlie also said that the Rainbow should consider some charity work or occasionally go to the church for guidance. The Rainbow agreed and thanked Charlie for his help and understanding. Charlie patted the Black n White Rainbow like a friendly dog and turned to leave. As he did so, the Rainbow smashed the mirror over Charlie's big pink head, knocking him to the ground. He then went on a second killing spree, much darker than the first.

THE END

USED JOHNYS

Conclusions:

The Rainbow had learnt nothing at all.

The moral of the story is:

Most people simply do not change.

Evil is rife in everyone and much more fun than doing good things for others.

Charlie died on the way to hospital and to make things worse he hadn't sorted out a will so his wife got nothing.

CHRISTY!

CHRISTY!

CHRISTY!

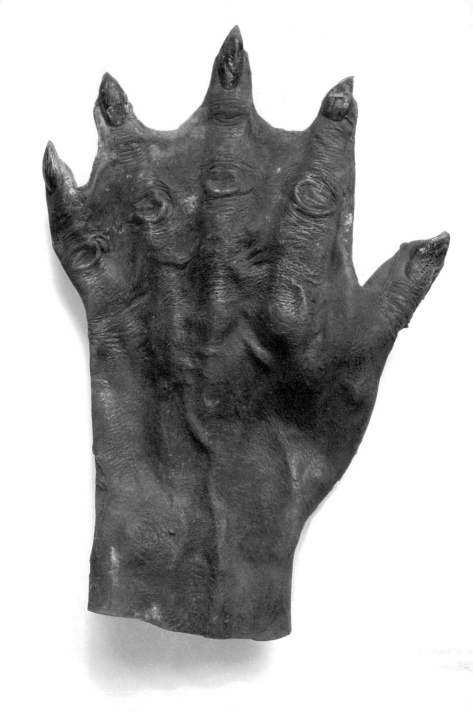

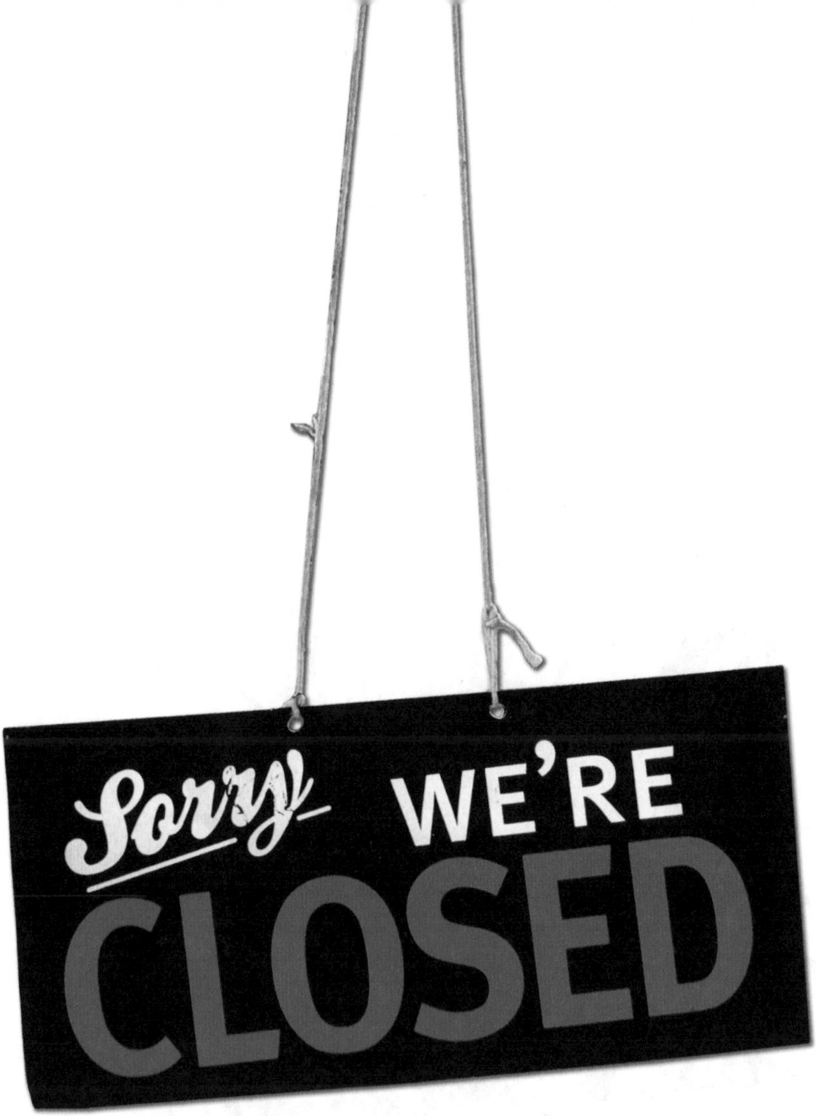
Sorry WE'RE
CLOSED

Dave would like to thank the following people for helping him make the Pocket Book of Boosh happen. In no particular order: Nick, Caroline, Jenny, Jamie and all at Canongate, Noel, Julian, Rich, Mike, Richard Ayoade, Ivana Zorn, Nige, Oli Ralfe, John Chandler, Jake, Jon Lee, Max, my lovely Lou, Andrew Rae, Andy Hollingworth, Mr Bingo, Tony Coppin, R&D&co, Nathan & Fibre, Christine Cant, Dee, Sue, June Nevin, Pete Stephens, Seano, Chiggy, Pat & PBJ, Steve Bell, Fraser & Nudie Jeans, Mark Hughes, Lambo, Reg Westlake, Susan, The mod wolves & all our lovely Fans
XXXXx